W9-BVQ-543

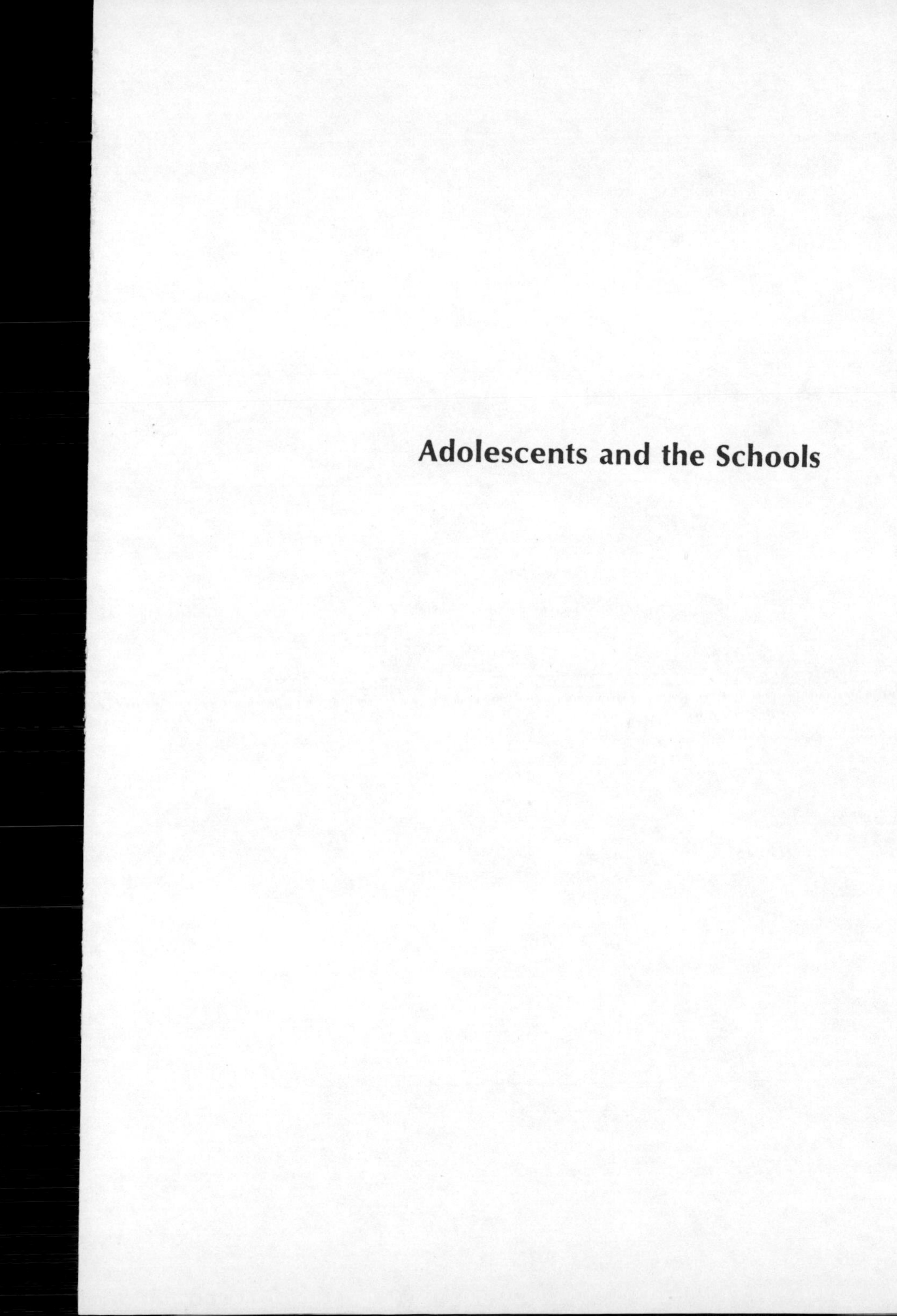

Adolescents and the Schools

Adolescents and the Schools

James S. Coleman

Basic Books, Inc., Publishers
New York London

SECOND PRINTING

Library of Congress Catalog Card Number: 65-21194
Manufactured in the United States of America
Designed by Linda Dean

Preface

Not many years ago, society was content largely to ignore education and to leave it in the hands of poorly paid teachers and principals. In so doing, we followed a long history of relative unconcern with the process of education. The Greeks, for example, whose interest in education surpassed that of almost any society, nevertheless showed remarkably little concern about the character of their children's schools and teachers. Schoolmasters were of low status and poorly paid, and tutors, even lower. Pericles is reported to have said, on seeing a slave fall from a tree and break his leg, "Lo, he is now a pedagogue."[1]

Part of the cause for society's lack of concern with the quality of education lies in the fact that schools have always been rather ancillary to the functioning society. The principal things most boys and all girls needed to know for their future occupation and civic life were learned within the family. In addition, the school's role has never been solely one of preparation but has always included custody—keeping the young occupied while adults went about important business.

It has finally become evident that education itself is important business; for those societies that are to survive, it must become

[1] E. B. Castle, *Ancient Education and Today* (New York: Penguin Books, 1961), p. 64.

a central concern. The entire rationalization and democratization of society has resulted in a child's no longer being able to learn from his parents the things he needs for his future. As a consequence, the task of shaping the members of the next generation falls progressively less on parents and more on society as a whole.

In recent years, there has been a growing body of informed discussion focused on matters of education. Much of this discussion has centered on a critical period that has always been the most ambiguous and ill-defined phase of education—secondary education. This period is best defined by exclusion: it follows primary education, at which the primary skills of literacy and basic calculation are taught; and it precedes the college years, which have traditionally been preparation for the professions.

The educational goals for the period of secondary education have often been unclear, as will be evident in Chapter 1, which briefly surveys the tortuous path that secondary education has followed in the United States. In addition, its clientele has been in an ambiguous state: between childhood and adulthood. Thus, of all education, it is secondary education that has been most beset by problems of what it should do and how to do it. The essays in this book give perspectives from three vantage points in an attempt to inform this discussion on education as it continues to grow.

Perhaps the most important perspective is a view inside the adolescent world. This world is increasingly becoming a world apart, with adolescent goals ill understood by adults and adult goals ill understood by adolescents. A view of the adolescent world reveals the kinds of constraint, pressure, and demand on an adolescent. It suggests how his potential may be frustrated or aided by his role as an adolescent, by the institutions (particularly the school) in which he is confined, and even by the adolescent social system that develops in such institutions. Chapters 2 and 3 take this perspective. Based on research into the adolescent subcultures in high schools, Chapter 2 examines the nature of these subcultures and their variations from school to school. Chapter 3 focuses on a particularly important element in the culture of adolescents and in the functioning of many schools, namely, athletics; it explores the role athletics plays for adolescents, for schools, and for communities.

But two other kinds of information are necessary. One concerns the most immediate problem to which a society's educational system must address itself: how to fill the economic roles that will keep the society functioning. Education has come to play a far more explicit part in the economic system than ever before. Today, it is not only the professions but an ever-widening range of occupations that require high levels of education. Information about the economy and its relation to education is in part a matter of numbers and rates of flow of persons through various kinds of training institution. It constitutes the hard-headed facts that are necessary for any informed discussion of social policy in education. Chapter 4 is addressed to this aspect of the problem. It assesses the current state of the American economy as it relates to education in an attempt to locate specific elements that might be changed to mesh these two systems more smoothly.

A final perspective that is necessary for informed discussion about secondary education concerns the very process and content of education. This is a longer-range view than either of the others, focusing on two fundamental problems. What should adolescents learn in order to be able to subsist in modern society, and how can education be so organized that they do come to learn this? Chapters 5 and 6 address these questions. As a preliminary to the discussion of these three perspectives, Chapter 1 points out some of the social changes that have occurred in American society in the past century and how these changes have influenced the content and structure of American education.

Throughout this book, my interest, indeed fascination, is with the adolescent. I view him as one of the last persons in modern society to be bound under a monolithic authority structure in one of the few remaining unfree (and thus irresponsible) roles in society.

Modern society, whether seen against the background of a feudal Europe of the Middle Ages or against the background of primitive society, has as its dominant direction the autonomy and independence of individuals. Society once consisted of an organization of authority relations. The household was the primary unit of economic production and consumption and had a hierarchy of dependency relations, with the head of the household as supreme authority. The transformations of society have been largely shifts toward autonomy. The movement from slavery or indentured servitude to wage labor was a major shift. The autonomy of women, still being won, is another major change. A third is the change in the role of children, a change that is occurring unevenly and is attended with many difficulties, from a subordinate role in the monolithic authority system of the family to one of relative independence.

Bringing children to adulthood was a simpler task for the adult society when children were obedient, content to be disciplined, and to see themselves and be seen as subordinates. But such children are the vanishing products of an earlier form of society. As they are replaced by adolescents who see themselves as autonomous, my moral values, which rebel against involuntary subordination wherever it may be found in society, and my aesthetic values, which find ultimate pleasure in a self-regulated society composed of self-regulated individuals, are both gratified.

I should indicate at the outset my conception of the adolescent. I do not see him as preoccupied with sexual problems, as such essayists as Paul Goodman and Eliot Friedenberg do. I accede that he has special problems with sexual expression, but

I suggest that these are magnified by the peculiar state of irresponsibility that is imposed on him. When sex is a dominant theme in adolescent life, it is for much the same reason it is at a cocktail party among adults: there is much free time and energy and no other goal to capture the imagination. I trust the adolescent to manage his affairs if he is given autonomy and opportunity.

I also do not see the adolescent as someone absorbed with discovery of a self, an identity, as, for example, J. D. Salinger does in his presentation of Holden Caulfield in *Catcher in the Rye*. To be sure, I recognize that morbid fascination with one's self is a preoccupation of youth (particularly those youth who are prevented from any responsible preoccupation with problems outside the self); and I recognize that at some point around adolescence many persons' identities do become established, an achievement sometimes attended by many difficulties. Yet, I do not think it appropriate that adults guide the adolescent through this difficult period; rather, I propose that he be given tools with which he, as an autonomous being, can fashion a self with the least permanent damage. These tools, I suggest, will allow the adolescent himself to conquer the morbid self-fascination with which he may be afflicted.

I do not see the major source of adolescent discontent to be the corruption of adult society. I see his discontent as akin to the discontent of the Negro in America and, like that discontent, to be a very hopeful sign. He, like the Negro, is impatient, not with the corruption of those in power, but with the fact that they have power over him.

If my interest is, as I have indicated above, wholly with freedom for adolescents, then my proposals should be rather simple ones: merely cast off the bonds of adult authority, and the children are free. Yet, this is clearly not what I propose. I am concerned, not merely about the present of the adolescent, but about his future. Thus, I want him to be free to act autonomously, but also to feel the consequences of that action so that he may learn for the future. The best learning has always proceeded in this way: one feels directly the consequences of his action and, if necessary, modifies his actions to make these consequences beneficial. The critical problem for the adolescent in modern society is that the consequences of his actions are indirect and far in the future; thus, they can have little impact on his current actions.

The traditional solution that adults have developed for this problem was quite simple: having seen the consequences themselves in their adulthood, they presumed to establish a "curriculum" or program which would be most beneficial to the adolescent's future. That is, they presumed to know the consequences and to decide what activities in the present would teach the adolescent to cope with the future. As long as adolescents were passively obedient and the future was enough like the past to make adults' decisions correct, this solution worked rather well—though it produced men whose obedience outran their spontaneity.

In the present, however, neither of these conditions holds, and their absence leads us to a far more appealing means by which adolescents can shape themselves for their future: give them freedom, but bring the future consequences into the present in order to make it possible for them to act knowing the consequences of that action. Such a possibility's appeal lies in the natural learning it induces; a child learns, not by being taught, but by finding himself in an environment that requires him to learn in order to survive.

Thus, the program that this solution implies is one of constructing environments. It is a program that says that an adolescent must be free to act as he wishes, but that society fails in its duty if it provides for his actions an environment which misleads him about the consequences.

The simplest way to provide such a misleading environment

is to do nothing at all, to let the adolescent act in his natural environment and feel only the immediate consequences. In modern society, such an environment can be very misleading indeed. The family solves his economic problems; thus he need never know that such problems exist. The family shelters him from the multiple legal and financial interactions it has with the outside society. He is never in the role of having to provide for others, so he cannot see life from this perspective. He is never in the role of one responsible for the supervision of others performing a task, so he never knows what the world looks like from this vantage point. This variety of roles is denied him. Thus his natural environment is not natural at all, but a sheltered and artificial one which prevents him from having contact with those very problems that can give him maturity.

The task, then, which I set as an ultimate goal, is to replace these artificial and sheltering environments with ones that reflect the consequences of the future. This is no easy task. It is a task that, once accomplished, allows the learning of adolescents to proceed in a way that prepares them for their future. In the past we have attempted the easy way, which purports to know what an adolescent should learn to prepare him for his environment as an adult and then attempts in courses to "teach" him. More and more that way is showing its inherent defects; adolescents no longer subject to the monolithic authority system of the family often show little interest in such offerings. Unimpressed with adults' judgments about what things they should learn, they are less and less patient to be "taught" these things. This artificial mode of learning becomes ever more inefficient and forces our attention toward alternatives more compatible with real learning.

JAMES S. COLEMAN

Baltimore, Maryland
July 1965

Contents

Adolescents and the Schools

1

Changes in Society and in Education

Social change has a way of perpetuating itself. Change in one part of society reverberates at other points, often having indirect effects at far removes. Henry Ford may have dreamed that his horseless carriage would revolutionize America's transportation, changing us from a nation of walkers to a nation of riders. But he certainly never dreamed that the automobile would change the entire urban structure of society, making suburbs out of farmlands and quickening the disintegration of the central city. Most certainly he could not have dreamed that his horseless carriage would drastically change the courting patterns of young America and that the back seat of Henry Ford's folly would supplant the parlor as the place where boys and girls become acquainted. Change at one point in society triggers a series of other changes. Yet, a society ordinarily waits–though these indirect effects are quite predictable if one pieces together the available information–until the effects are manifest before taking account of them. To phrase it differently, sociologists sometimes talk of the "unanticipated consequences" of social change. The task of a society faced with rapid change is to anticipate these indirect consequences, to air them and, hopefully, to stimulate action concerning them.

Concurrent changes can have a joint effect that is quite unexpected. Consider the rapid suburbanization of our society, which for present purposes means only that there is a movement of the city's population out of the city's single school system and uniform school taxes into small local systems, each financed by the local community. Then, consider the effect of both suburbanization and the high birth rate: the need for new and larger schools, which creates a special tax burden. Finally, consider these suburban communities in the light of modern transportation; they are frequently only places to *live* and not places to *work*. They are bedroom communities, often lacking any industry. The place of work is dissociated from the place of residence, creating highly homogeneous and strictly residential communities.

What does a combination of these changes produce? First, local rather than central school systems; second, the need for expanded school facilities; and, third, one-class nonindustrial communities. The joint effect is a gross inequality in school financing, with a few suburbs very well off and many suffering badly. How and why? A concrete example will clarify this.

There are two high schools in Oaklawn, a community in southwest suburban Chicago. One district includes nothing but rows of new lower-middle-class houses. The other includes similar rows of houses, but with one added feature—the Clearing Industrial District, composed of industries that together pay a major portion of the school district's taxes. The first school district can hardly maintain itself, much less expand to meet the increased birth rate and the influx of new residents; the second can afford luxurious facilities and well-paid teachers. This example should illustrate my point that concurrent changes in society can have joint effects that are not predictable when each change is examined by itself.

Economic and Educational Changes

The first set of changes I want to discuss requires a tracing of the history of secondary education in this country and the forces that have shaped it from the beginning.[1] Until late in the nineteenth century, public education was primarily an elementary school matter. Preparation for college was done by private secondary schools and a few public schools. For example, in 1870, there were only 800 public high schools in this country. Although the number rapidly increased from that time, high school education continued to be oriented to the few young people going to college. In 1900, only 11 per cent of the high school aged population was in school. High school was for a minority of the population; it was designed for those going to college, as attested by the fact that two-thirds of the graduates did go on to college—a higher rate than at any time since. High school was for the "educated class"; it was a direct descendant of the European secondary schools that prepared for the professions—the English grammar school, the French *lycée*, and the German *Gymnasium*.[2] Farm boys left school before or directly after the eighth grade to help full time on the farm. Workers' sons left to take up a trade and begin an apprenticeship.

There were essentially two societal institutions influencing these early high schools. Colleges could dictate the standards by which they would accept the high schools' products. For example, the National Education Association appointed a committee to determine history curricula for high schools. Six of the seven committee members were historians—college history pro-

[1] See Charles R. Keller, "Origins and History of the Secondary School," *College Admissions*, 6 (1959), 1–9.

[2] The European secondary schools, when faced with economic changes similar to those that took place in American society, responded in a somewhat different way. Rather than transforming the secondary school to cover a larger part of the population, they established parallel, nonacademic schools, maintaining in pristine form the university preparatory school. Thus, even now, a small minority attends academic secondary schools, comparable to the 11 per cent that, in 1900, attended American schools. Yet, the lack of opportunity for the lower classes that this imposes and its inability to provide the mass education required for a modern economy are creating pressures for comprehensive schools. Such pressure is particularly manifest in England.

fessors. The NEA, in effect, was asking the colleges to design the preparation they desired for their entrants. The report of this committee, issued in 1897, dictated four specific years of history; it had a powerful impact on textbooks and curricula. Thus, the high school at its start was tightly tied to the college, and the standards of colleges largely dictated the form that high school education would take.

The other institution that shaped the early high school was the family, which fed the high school its material. It was not the "average American family" that pressured the school, but a highly selected family–selected because of its college aims for its children. These were families, in short, who were strongly in favor of education. Thus, from both directions, the high school in its formative stage was molded into a college preparatory school. The colleges set the standards, and the family helped to enforce them.

What kind of teacher did such a system imply? Teachers well schooled in the academic subjects of college; teachers whose primary concern was the content of what they were teaching and who were only secondarily concerned with the students being taught. If a child would not learn, he need not stay in school; his very presence implied a commitment on his or his parents' part toward learning. Thus, a teacher did not need to know how to teach; he only needed to know his subject. This is not to say that these content-oriented teachers would not have profited by teaching-methods training; it can only be said that, with highly motivated, voluntarily present students, they could–and did–get along without it.

But social changes were affecting secondary education. Industrialization did away with the apprenticeship training and gave working-class boys nothing to do until they were old enough and strong enough for factory labor. Industrialization also expanded the number of white-collar jobs that required high school training–clerks, salesmen, accountants, office workers of all kinds. Increasing prosperity made both farmers' and workers' families less dependent on their children's labor.

Society no longer needed the labor of children, so it passed child labor laws, removing them from the working force. Since it could not have free-roaming children, it committed them to an institution where they could be kept out of the way and, hopefully, some of them would be trained for the new white collar jobs. What institution? The public high school, of course. High school education shifted from a voluntary matter for the few going to college to an involuntary matter for all. The statistics are startling. In 1900, 11 per cent of the high school aged population was in school; in 1920, 32 per cent; in 1930, 51 per cent; in 1940, 73 per cent; and today, about 90 per cent.

This great shift in numbers greatly modified the forces impinging on the high school. The high schools' products were no longer destined for college, but largely for industry and business. As the proportion of teen-agers in high school grew, the proportion of graduates attending college dropped from two-thirds in 1900 to about half in 1920 to about a third in 1940. Thus the majority were directly going into jobs, and the college requirements were no longer the sole basis of the high school curriculum. Industry's needs had to be attended to as well, giving rise to "practical" courses: industrial arts, shops, typing, and others.

There was a concomitant change in the families feeding the high school; they were no longer an educated elite with sons and daughters destined for college. Everyone was included: some interested in education, others only tolerant of it; some with highly motivated children, others with "slow learners."

What did these changes imply for curriculum and teacher training? Neither the curriculum nor the teacher could be solely concerned with college preparation. The very function of a high school education became different, as attested by the seven cardinal principles of secondary education issued in 1918 by an

NEA committee, a very different committee from the 1897 one: health, command of fundamental mental processes, worthy home-membership, vocation, civic education, worthy use of leisure, and ethical character. Thus, in content, high school shifted in a nonacademic direction: from college preparation to life adjustment. In method, far more concern with motivation was necessary. A high school became a place of involuntary confinement for many students, and an important task for teachers was to make it less involuntary, to convince students that school was worthwhile. The typical high school teacher changed from an austere academician (who may have intended to become a college teacher and who in fact might someday become one) to an attentive and sympathetic teacher, trained as much in method as in subject matter, schooled in educational psychology and group dynamics. He or she was quite unlikely ever to move to college teaching–and, in fact, may never have seen the inside of a liberal arts college but only those special institutions called teachers' colleges.

This is essentially the current state of affairs. The curriculum is designed for the entire community, not just for college-bound students, and teachers' problems center as much on motivation as on the subject matter. There are, of course, wide variations. Some communities are almost entirely made up of college-bound students; others send few children to college.

Social changes have continued in ways that have important implications for high schools and for the training of teachers. The industrial revolution has continued and has, first of all, created an ever-increasing amount of leisure. Again, it is the young whose labor is unnecessary. Not only are they not needed after the eighth grade, they are not needed after high school. So college training becomes a requirement or at least an important asset for more and more jobs. Secondly, as industrialization proceeds, there are fewer laboring jobs, fewer routine clerical jobs, and more jobs which require academic training beyond high school.

Consequently, more and more eighteen-year-olds go to college rather than to a job. The proportion of high school graduates entering college has reversed the steady decline it experienced from 1900 to the 1940's, and there is every indication that it will continue to increase. There is every reason to believe that college attendance will grow at a rate paralleling that of the high schools from 1900 to the present. What this means for high schools, of course, is that, with more graduates attending college, more students will require preparation for college rather than seek a terminal education. More specifically, there are three current changes that combine to have important implications: college is becoming the destination of more high school graduates; competition for a place in good colleges is sharply increasing and will continue to do so; college admission policies are increasingly based on an applicant's ability and on the quality of high school training.

The implications of these changes are fairly straightforward. As the proportion of high school graduates entering college rises, the concern of parents with their child's getting into the "right" school increases. In one suburban school I studied, 85 per cent of the graduates entered college. There is a heavy emphasis on choosing and getting into the "right" college. A student's consultations with his homeroom teacher about college begin in his freshman year and continue until a choice is made and acceptance is certain. The parents closely examine the success of their children's high school as compared to neighboring ones in placing students in "good" colleges. In contrast, other communities have few graduates attending college. A parent's pride is more easily satisfied; a child will be outstanding even by attending college.

As more high schools reach a high level of 70–90 per-cent college-bound graduates, competition for prestigeful schools will increase. The consequences for the school and for teacher education are clear: more pressure will be exerted for good college preparation. More schools will develop accelerated programs to enable their graduates to compete for the top colleges. Accelerated courses—and courses in general—will require teachers who know a lot about their subject matter. There will be pressure from the communities on state boards of education to decrease teachers' requirements in education or to make wholesale exceptions so that schools can get subject-matter specialists from liberal arts colleges. The pressure will be on the teachers' colleges as well—that is, it will increase, for the pressure has already begun —to strengthen their subject-matter training, to produce, not "teachers," but historians, mathematicians, physicists, social scientists, and scholars of English literature.

Changes in the Social Organization of Adolescence

I seem to be saying that social changes are forcing a return to the austere academician concerned only with the subject. Then education will have come full cycle, from academy to life adjustment and back to academy. But things are not as simple as this, for there are other important social changes that have distinctly different implications—not for curriculum as much as for method. The changes are these:

(1) For a variety of reasons, teen-agers are becoming socially sophisticated earlier than ever before. They simply *know* more about the world, more about sex and about the opposite sex, and have more opportunity to learn both academic and nonacademic matters outside of school. Exposure to radio, television, movies, and books is making children wiser in the ways of the world than the children of an earlier age. I do not mean to say that this sophistication has made them more serious and more responsible; there are forces in the opposite direction. It has, however, made them less in awe of adults, less willing to listen to a teacher just because he is a teacher.

(2) Now, more than ever before, the school encompasses the

total community of adolescents. A boy's friends are confined to his schoolmates, because everyone his age is in school. The adolescent's social sphere has become the social system of the high school. To be sure, this change has been manifest for some time, for high school has encompassed the majority of teen-agers for many years. But its full consequences for the educational process have not been recognized.

(3) To reinforce this setting-apart of the school as a separate social system, there is less need for the adolescent in the adult world. His family duties, whether on the farm, around the house, or in his father's store, are evaporating. The father no longer owns a farm or store but works in an office or a factory where his son cannot help at all. And labor-saving devices for housewives have, as a by-product, made the aid of a daughter unnecessary in cooking, in sewing, in keeping house. She is cast out on her own, to "have fun" with her friends. Parenthetically, I should note the universal importance of "having fun" or "having a good time" among adolescents in high school. This is a characteristic of bad students and good ones, of rock-and-rollers and honor-rollers. It is a further indication of their isolation from responsibility in the adult society, an indication of the degree to which the adult world has found them economically unnecessary and thus, unwittingly, told them to "go have fun" with their friends.

(4) A further reinforcement of the social world of adolescents has been the emergence of commercial entertainment designed specifically for them. Popular music is the best example; movies are another, particularly since adult patrons have been largely lost to television.

(5) With all of these factors making for a special world of teen-agers, there is one other very important point: they must go to school. Education is compulsory through most of high school, and compulsory education is very different from voluntary education. Motivation shifts from learning to "getting by," until

teacher and students alike become satisfied with fulfilling formal requirements rather than teaching and learning.

The combination of these five changes has produced a peculiar set of circumstances: adolescents have their own little society, with special symbols and language, special interests and activities. It is a society composed of people who are worldly-wise in many ways, of people who are more adult than child, yet a society of people without responsibilities, a society subject to the demands placed on it by others—that is, by adults. To be sure, adults are doing this for their "own good," but it is the adult who decides what is good and what is not. Such a situation invites trouble. It encourages leadership that asserts itself against the adult demands. It encourages a disdain for those who exert extra effort to meet adult demands. It encourages a status system among adolescents based on such extra-school activities as dating and sports. In sum, it effectively impedes education, keeping the effort expended on learning at a minimum.

Yet, despite the importance of these changes, changes that have presented schools with a tightly knit and sometimes suspicious society of semi-adults, there has been little recognition of them in educational philosophies. Classical education, progressive education, and all their variants have never faced the problem that bedevils society now: how to deal with a group that confronts the school as a group, not as a set of discrete individuals. How can a school or a teacher motivate an entire social system toward learning when its natural tendency is opposition to such seriousness and when it no longer conceives of the teacher as an omniscient authority?

2

Style and Substance in American Education

It is surprisingly difficult to find people who have a comprehensive view of high schools and who can give a broad picture of the differences among them. Most adults never set foot in a high school once they graduate; and secondary school people themselves are often engrossed in the one institution with which they are involved and have a kind of worm's eye view, not knowing how other high schools differ from their own.

But a search will reveal people who have a real awareness of the differences among schools. There are a few researchers, such as Paul R. Mort, who devoted much of his career to charting differences among high schools throughout the country. And within each state, there are men with special experiences; for example, state assistant superintendents of schools who periodically visit each school in their state, public and private, to check facilities for accreditation. But some who have this awareness turn up in unexpected situations: basketball referees who referee games througout a particular area feel some of the intangible differences among its high schools. The referees cannot tell you how good the school's physics department is, but they do know how high the basketball fever rages and how many hot-rodders there are in each school; and they frequently have a sensitive finger on the pulse of juvenile delinquency at different schools.

I think it would be a fine tonic for American secondary education if school principals and headmasters were uprooted for a few weeks every year or so to attend classes and teachers' meeting in high schools other than their own. As it is, few communication links connect these separate islands, each with its own culture and its own natives trying to solve identical problems. America's largest corporation, American Telephone and Telegraph, has handled a similar communication problem in an ingenious way. It conducted a management attitude survey through all sixteen operating Bell Telephone Companies. When the results were in, a vice president of a company generally low on the survey and a vice president of a company that came out high were sent as a team to observe the two companies and to write a report on the differences they found.

My experience, covering only a few schools and their variations, has been more like that of the AT & T observers than of the state assistant superintendent, with his panoramic view of one thousand schools. But this narrower focus allows an intensive look at some of the differences that do show up among the schools and suggests some questions about the existing situation.

First of all, I want to discuss differences in *substance*, that is, in the content of the education that the schools present. But secondly, I want to examine what might be called differences in *style* of education among schools. What I mean by this is the kind of orientation toward college, toward learning, and toward intellectual activity with which a boy or girl leaves high school. This is not in any sense the same as the amount of information he has, nor is it his level of academic achievement; it is his attitude toward further achievement. As such, it is an important key to his accomplishment in job or college, perhaps a more important key than his present level of achievement in English, algebra, or whatever. Far too often, such differences in orientation are looked on as purely the individual responsibility of the student himself.

I want to suggest, however, that differences in orientation

toward learning are just as much a product of a high school education as are the concrete facts a boy or girl knows at the end of high school. I remember, when I was in high school, wishing intensely that the teachers would not destroy in us all desire to learn, and wanting to make a pact with them somehow by saying, "Look, I don't care if you don't teach us anything. Just leave intact the curiosity and inquisitiveness we had when we came to school."

The third matter I want to examine is *why* such differences in substance and in style exist. What elements are there in the schools and the communities that generate the seventeen-year-old specimens with whom colleges and businesses must contend?

Types of School

The information and ideas I have on these subjects stem largely from differences among ten high schools.[1] These ten schools are all in the Midwest, but there the similarity stops. One of the high schools has less than one hundred students; two of the others have about two thousand each. One of the schools is a Catholic boys' school in the heart of a big-city slum, struggling along with inadequate equipment and large classes. Four of the schools are small town schools in the three-hundred to five-hundred student range. One of these four was vividly described in *Elmtown's Youth*,[2] which portrays the school as it was in 1941—a hidebound, small town Midwestern school surrounded by farms and coal mines, a school in which a lower-class child had no chance and in which the favored middle-class children received a poor education at best. Things have changed somewhat in Elmtown. It

[1] These schools were subjects in a study I conducted in 1957–1958, under a grant from the United States Office of Education. In some places I will quote from interviews with students made in an extension of this study, carried out by Peter Rossi and myself, under a grant from the College Entrance Examination Board.

[2] August B. Hollingshead (New York: John Wiley & Sons, Inc., 1949).

has a new high school building and a new principal, and the town is more prosperous. But some things have stayed the same, which I shall discuss later.

One school, with a student body of two thousand, is a comprehensive high school in a two-school city of 150,000 population. Another is a new school in a homogeneous working-class suburb where few of the students' parents ever finished college. Still another is a school in a wealthy suburb which sends between 80 and 90 per cent of all its graduates to college. On the basis of the number of National Merit Scholarships its students have won, this high school ranks among the top schools in the country. Along with a few other schools in this area, it is a Midwestern analog of the well-endowed Westchester County suburban school—perhaps even more luxurious. In the Midwest, the institution of the private boarding school just doesn't exist as it does in the East. In most well-to-do Midwestern suburbs practically none of the students are siphoned off to private schools. Instead, upper-middle-class parents endow their public schools with excellent facilities and faculties and a rich curriculum, and then send their children to them.

This school is an extreme example of the plush public high schools that have been blossoming forth in upper-middle-class suburban communities in recent years. These schools look like the wave of the future to some educators when they examine present-day population shifts to the suburbs and income shifts to the upper middle class.

These are some of the more obvious differences in the facilities and resources that these schools possess. In many respects these differences are as great as night and day, and all within a radius of two hundred miles. For example, in the year 1955–56, the plush suburban school spent over $700 on each of its pupils and built a lavish new school plant as well. That same year, one of the small town schools spent less than half as much for each of its pupils, who continued to study in the same small, inadequate building their fathers and mothers had attended.

I want to discuss first the differences in *substance* to which the title of this chapter refers, the difference in the substance of things learned. The schools' differences in facilities naturally reflect themselves in the quality of education they are able to give their students. An example of these differences is the number of English courses available to seniors. In the comprehensive school (in a light industry city of about 150,000) there are four different English courses available for college-bound seniors. In the plush suburban school, the college-bound seniors have five English courses to choose from and may take more than one at a time if they like. In the smallest school, by contrast, there is only one English teacher, one English class for seniors, and hardly enough students in this class to justify giving it.

In one of the schools, I observed a class in human biology where the students were determining the Rh factors in each other's blood. The next week, they were to take a trip to the state psychiatric hospital and later were to receive twenty-four calves' hearts from the stockyards for dissection. This class did not use one biology text; it used five, all of them college textbooks. I shall return to the discussion of this biology class later; it was neither in the plush suburban school nor in the comprehensive city school with the four senior English courses.

These differences in the quality of things taught are paralleled by differences in the study habits of the children. In the smallest of the small town schools, less than 10 per cent of the boys reported studying more than an hour on an average weeknight. Furthermore, the number studying this much decreased from the freshman class through the four years, so that not a single senior boy reported studying more than an hour a night. At the other extreme, in the plush suburban school, more than 50 per cent of the boys (and about 80 per cent of the girls) reported studying over an hour each weeknight.

These differences might be expected, but some of the others are not so easily explained. The next to smallest of the ten schools is located near the smallest school and in a very similar community. Yet in this school almost five times as many students study over an hour each night as do in the neighboring community. This is not so many as in the plush suburban school, but not very far from it. And in contrast to its neighbor, in the next to smallest school, the proportion of students studying at night increases over the four years from freshman to senior.

Among the boys in the poorly equipped parochial school located in the slum district, the proportion of after-school studying is equally high—it is third among the ten schools. Here, too, the amount of studying goes up over the four years of school. A quick survey of the other schools shows a wide variation, with the boys in the small town schools generally—but not always—doing less studying at home than boys in the city schools.

Let us take a closer look at the different grades in the well-to-do suburban school; the freshmen study more than the seniors do. The time devoted to studying goes down over the four years among the boys in this school. Such a result is a little disquieting; it seems inconsistent with the general picture this school presents and suggests that we investigate matters a little more closely. In doing so, we shall be shifting from substance to style, from the content of what is taught and learned to the orientation toward learning itself. Just what kind of orientation to learning do these schools leave with their graduates?

To begin to answer such a question requires us to move to the world of the adolescents themselves, to look at them in the context of all their interests and activities, and to ask how big a part school work plays.

The Teen-agers' World

A shock awaits the adult who makes his first venture into the present-day world of adolescents. He finds it populated with jazzed-up autos, athletic stars, and "the group," that most powerful agent in a teen-ager's life, which calls him to go for a ride, or to go down to the snack bar, or just to come and "hang around." But is this the world of the college-bound teen-ager? Let us see.

In every school there is a "leading crowd." This is not so strange. Every community of adults has its leading crowd, its elite (although adults less often find themselves in such close and compelling communities as do adolescents in a high school). In some schools there is more than one group competing for power; and some schools are large enough to support two or more, just as some adult communities are large enough to support two or more elites. But in each of these ten schools, agreement was fairly universal about who the members of the respective leading crowds were. In more than half of these schools, the elite consisted in large part of college-bound boys and girls.

What does it take to get into the leading crowd in these schools? This is another way of asking what the dominant values are in these adolescent cultures. According to the adolescents themselves (and we asked all of them this question) it takes a lot of things; but academic success is not one of them. It takes athletic prowess, knowing how to dance, owning a car, having a good reputation, or liking to have fun. It takes being a good date, liking parties, and often not being a prude (for girls) or a sissy (for boys). Good grades and intelligence are mentioned, but not very often, and not as often as any of the other items.

This is an oversimplification, of course, because the students in these schools differed widely in their values. In one school, as much as 20 per cent of the boys and 20 per cent of the girls spontaneously mentioned good grades (or "having brains") as a criterion for being in the leading crowd. Which school was this? Not the plush suburban school with its excellent facilities and staff, but the comprehensive city school. Good grades are valued next highest in the parochial school, populated by lower-class boys whose parents emigrated from eastern Europe. Third in line is the small town school in which the students—sons and daughters of farmers and villagers–spend much time in nightly study. The plush suburban school, with the sons and daughters of professionals and business executives, is close to the bottom for the boys, though somewhat higher for the girls, in the value that students place on good grades. It stands alongside a small town school dominated by football and alongside Elmtown's school.

Is this an accident, a freak occurrence, resulting from the way the question was asked? Suppose we take a different tack: who are the popular heroes in these schools? That is, whom in school would the boys (or girls) like to emulate? Whom would they most like to have as a friend? We asked each student both these questions. We also asked who in the school was the best athlete (for girls, who was the best dressed), who was the best student, and who was most popular with the opposite sex. Now suppose we compare their answers to the first two questions with the answers to the last three. This way we can see, in a fairly subtle fashion, just what kinds of values their popular heroes exemplify. How often is the best athlete the person they would most like to be like or be friends with? How often is the best student this person? And how often is it the boy or girl who is most popular with the opposite sex?

Here again the general values of adolescent culture are evident. Either the athletes or the lady-killers (and in most schools, both) outdistance the best students. But how do the best students in the plush suburban school, with its extraordinary facilities and its many National Merit Scholarships, fare as popular heroes in comparison to the best students in the other school? The popular heroes in the plush suburban school are the boys whom the girls "go for" most. This school stands first among all the schools in the number of boys wanting to be friends with the boys most popular with girls, and seventh in the number of boys wanting to be friends with the best students. It stands alongside the small town football-oriented school again, this time below Elmtown's school.

The pattern of choice is true for freshmen, sophomores, juniors, and seniors, and is similar among the girls of this school. Their popular heroines are divided between the best-dressed girls and the ones the boys like most. Few of the girls pick the best girl student as their idol.

There are other criteria, and the suburban school is consistent on all of them: if you ask a boy if he wants to be remembered in this school as a brilliant student, a star athlete, or the most popular, only 25 per cent will answer "as a brilliant student"; an even smaller percentage prevails for girls. If you ask a boy or girl which type of student he or she would like to date, the number choosing the brilliant student goes down to around 10 per cent. If you ask the boys how they would spend an extra hour at school if they had it, only about one-quarter of them would spend it on a course of their own choosing, or in the study hall. Twice as many would spend it in athletics. If you ask the boys whether they would rather be a nationally famous athlete or an atomic scientist, many more would prefer to be a nationally famous athlete.

All this is surprising enough, yet even more surprising is that, in each of these criteria relating to the value placed on scholastic achievement, the surburban school, with its preponderance of sons and daughters of professionals and business executives, stands near the bottom of the list—anywhere from seventh to tenth among the ten schools.

Which school stands near the top most consistently? It is the small town, academically oriented school. This school combines a wide range of diversity in itself. The star athlete of the senior class is a likable farm boy whose real interest is in raising fighting chickens and staging cockfights. I thought I heard him incorrectly when he answered a question about his interests by saying "I fight chickens." He was planning to race greyhounds in Florida until he got offers from three universities for his football ability. At the other extreme in this school is the outstanding student in the junior class—a boy who says he gets "a charge" out of arguing philosophy with his father, a local lawyer. This boy decided, after carefully reading the *Harvard Register*, that he will try to go to Harvard; he is impressed by the house system there, for he thinks he can learn more that way.

Who Sets the Tone?

The difference between this academically oriented school and some of its unacademically inclined neighbors is perhaps simple to understand; this school manages to let the boy with the *Harvard Register* set the tone for the others—and it puts the *Harvard Register* in his hands in the first place.

Its nonacademically inclined neighbor school, in contrast, lets the star athlete set the tone and helps him to do so, in ways that one of our interviews with a senior at the school illustrates:

"I think a lot of the trouble with the whole school is in the athletic program."

"How do you mean?"

"Well, unfortunately, the athletic director pretty well dominated the administration.[3] Too many of the boys took everything he said for the gospel truth. He was one of the people who made some remark about our class when we were freshmen. He said that as far as students were concerned, we were good students, but that was about all, implying that we weren't good athletes. He said it in our general science class. He implied that we were sissified."

When I visited this school in the fall and talked to the senior English class (a class for college-bound seniors), I joked about their lack of success in football and was met by a wall of blank stares. It was not funny; this senior class had developed a feeling of inferiority, a defensive attitude, because the boys in their class

[3] The administration had changed the year before.

were not good athletes. Why did they develop this defensiveness? Because the rewards in this school were for athletic prowess.

The other schools varied widely in the kinds of attitude their students had toward learning. By all the criteria mentioned above, students in the parochial school, the comprehensive city school, and one of the other small town schools showed a relatively strong desire to study, while students' impetus toward study in the two other small town schools was relatively weak. In the working-class suburb, it is not so much a question of whether the athletes or the good students will constitute the leading crowd, but rather whether the star athletes or the most daring delinquents will capture the imagination of the students.

One of the surprising results is the high academic orientation of the students in the parochial boys' school, located in the city slum. Lacking many of the facilities of even the most outdated small town schools and certainly unable to transmit a quality of education comparable to the best of the others, it nevertheless has created a student body who look to the best students for their leadership. It may be argued that this is due to the lack of other activities, in contrast to the abundance of clubs, athletics, and other extracurricular enterprises that flourish at the luxurious suburban school and some of the other schools with elaborate facilities. Perhaps so, and perhaps this is precisely the point: the students of the plush suburban school are surrounded by a school environment in which academic activity is only one small part. A wealth of other interests can gain their attention and shift the limelight away from success in school studies.

There are a number of indications that the absence of one factor in particular in the parochial school has a lot to do with its more academic orientation. There are no girls here as there are in each of the other schools. The presence of girls in a school has a powerful impact on the directions toward which boys focus their energies, and it is obvious that this impact may not always be a salutary one. This is particularly so when a school encompasses a large part of its students' social activities, as is the style now in many suburban schools. Boy–girl relationships come to play an important part in the social system of the school. It is no accident, and should come as no surprise, that the boys in the plush suburban school most often pick as the boy they want to be like the boy whom they think the girls like most.

It may be argued that boys who go to a school without girls will become socially and psychologically maladjusted, completely unprepared for a normal adult life—but I doubt it. As a matter of fact, the boys and girls in the coeducational schools may be more twisted psychologically by the power that social cliques exert in their schools. No person is more desolate than a teen-age girl excluded from the crowd she aspires to. I think this sort of social exclusion hurts most in the suburban schools, which encompass such a large part of the lives of their students. The proportion of all students who said they would like to be in the leading crowd in school was high in all schools, but highest in the suburban school.

The curious fact in all this is that these differences in "style" among the schools are not more closely related to differences in substance. We all begin by assuming that they are. We assume that good facilities and good teachers will capture the imagination and attention of a boy or girl. But this assumption ignores the fact that there may be other things competing for his attention. Of all the ten schools we studied, a child probably can receive the best education, the most content for his four years of effort, in the wealthy suburban school.

If a boy or girl attending this school desires, he or she can easily outdistance the student of comparable ability in most of the other schools. And to be sure, many of them do, as their study habits indicate. Yet, ask these same good students which boy or girl in their school they most want to be like, and they will tell you the name of the student whom they think the opposite sex "goes for" most. The orientation toward learning of these suburban seniors is far below that of the college-bound seniors in the small town school with the academic climate, the comprehensive city school, and the slum-district parochial school.

A sense of this is obtained by comparing an interview with the valedictorian of the suburban school with excerpts from an interview with the valedictorian of the comprehensive city school. We asked the suburban senior: "What impressed you most about the college you're going to attend?"

He answered, "Well, when I think about it, I remember where I stayed when I visited there—I stayed with these two boys—we stayed in the freshman dormitory. They were nice guys, I liked them. I recall that, and I think of the fraternity house. I visited some classrooms, but that's not what stuck in my mind."

Later, we asked, "What was the most important influence on your choice of Cornell, Michigan, and Harvard?"

His response was prompt: "Well, I guess I chose them rather than Southern Illinois or something like that because these are big schools; they have a fine reputation. I know that if I say to someone, 'I'm a graduate of Michigan, or Cornell, or Harvard,' that they'd say, 'That's a good school, you must be on the ball!' "

This boy, like his classmates, wanted more to be *from* a particular college than to get something *out of* it.

Compare this with the attitude of the valedictorian from the less well-endowed city school. We asked, "Why did you decide on Harvard?"

He replied, "As you know, it has the reputation of being the best in the country, and I liked the atmosphere of a small college, which it is supposed to have, with its house system. On the other hand, I liked the facilities of a large university. And then I liked the entire climate out there—the intellectual part of it."

This boy was one of a group of strong political conservatives in the school, a group that held violent political arguments with a group of girls who were equally strong liberals, and who made up the leading crowd of girls in this school.

These interviews were quite informal. We asked the students

a few questions about their college plans and then let them talk about the things that interested them. In looking at the transcripts of most of the interviews we held in the plush suburban school, one must flip through several pages before coming to the point where the content of a college education comes up. It is preceded by talk of fraternities and sororities, friends that can be made in college, and above all, the problems of getting into the "right" school. One gets the impression that these students and their parents have been so concerned about the problems of getting into the right college that they have nearly forgotten what a college education is about. The students' concern with being accepted by the right college seems to have occupied whatever energies they had left over from their social activities.

Student attitudes toward various "off-beat" colleges are a good test of the intellectual climate that permeates a school. The University of Chicago is one such school for these Midwestern seniors. In some of the small town and city schools, students had sent away for University of Chicago catalogues and were considering going there. They didn't know any better—all they were after was an education. In the plush suburban school, the University of Chicago was almost never on the list of students' college choices, because it was felt that it would not create the same social effect to be from Chicago as it would to be from Yale.

I think something of the same spirit pervades the climate of many private schools. I talked later to a girl who would be a senior the next year in an elite girls' school in Connecticut. She was considering going to Oberlin, but added that the other girls in her group could not understand her. Just two eastern women's colleges were *the* colleges; a girl was foolish not to try for one of them. She was already wavering because her choice was so divergent from the norm.

Right College, Wrong Reason

Perhaps this difference among schools can be summed up this

way; in some highly privileged schools the students go to the right colleges, but for the wrong reasons. In many small isolated high schools the students have the right reasons, but they end in the wrong colleges.

This last point, that some good students choose the wrong colleges, is perhaps most disquieting of all. I recently looked through questionnaires filled out by all the National Merit Scholars of 1957, concerning their reasons for selecting the college they did. Some of these statements are upsetting for the first-mentioned reason; they show a boy or girl going to the right college for the wrong reasons. But some are distressing for the opposite reason: they show a boy or girl choosing an inferior college because he or she has never seen a glimpse of any other. Let me give you an example of what I mean. A bright young girl who chose to attend a very small college, wrote:

"I have many interests and the college of my choice offers a very comprehensive course, written and taught by a member of their faculty, called Civilization. This college is the only one that can offer this course, and I feel that it will give me a chance to learn a little about many subjects I am interested in without sacrificing any of my main courses."

Consider also the male junior in the small town who is now planning to go to Harvard, the boy I spoke of earlier who "gets a charge" out of discussing philosophy. He had intended to go to the state university his father had attended, until his English teacher required a research theme on plans after high school. This started him looking in reference books and sending away for college catalogues; and in this way he was introduced to other colleges. But the point is, he had to *look*—no one came to him. No visiting representatives of Eastern colleges and few representatives of out-of-state colleges came to his high school at all.

In contrast, the comprehensive city school and the plush suburban school have to shoo away the college visitors. As if this were not enough, many of the parents of the children have told them far more about college and colleges than they would learn any other way. They will apply to four or five schools each (as many as their high school will allow); the small town Harvard aspirant will probably apply only to Harvard, not knowing any better.

Let us make another comparison. Take the athletic star from the same small town school. How did he get his ideas on where to apply to college? Here is a little of his interview.

We asked: "How long have you planned to go to college?"

His answer: "Last semester, since I got this football recognition and track recognition, colleges became interested in me right away." The colleges, incidentally, were not local colleges; they were the universities of Indiana, Illinois, and Tennessee.

So, while the athletic star of the small town school is discovered immediately, the brilliant student at the same school must ferret out information as best he can. And then the question of acceptance is not his choice, as it is for the athletic star; it is the college's. It is almost as if colleges were answering the question, "Which would you rather accept—the brilliant student or the athletic star?" And the colleges, like the high school boys themselves, are choosing the athletic stars.

I have heard of only one action on the part of colleges toward a star student comparable to the athletic talent scouting and scholarship offers directed at high school football stars. In one of the small schools we studied, a senior who had placed fairly high in the National Merit Scholarship examination (but not high enough for a Merit scholarship) was sought out by a number of small colleges, which made him scholarship offers, just as the state universities made offers to the high school football star. These offers made the student realize for the first time what was available to him in the way of colleges beyond a fifty-mile radius. He was still not as well-informed as the students in the large city and suburban schools, but his ignorance about colleges had diminished considerably. A few colleges, incidentally, are using

National Merit Scholarship finalists to transform their student body quickly by offering scholarships to these students.

This is all I shall say about the differences in style and substance that exist among these high schools with which I am familiar. The differences in substance are obvious, and I have devoted little space to them; the differences in style are less obvious, and I have devoted much space trying to make them and their consequences a little more obvious. Now let us examine why these differences occur.

First, why is athletics so important in so many schools, particularly in towns with only one or two high schools? Why is it that a small town high school principal often has to work hard to keep the atmosphere of his school from being dominated by athletics?

I think the reason lies more with the adult community than we realize. Athletic contests represent more to a community than mere sports competition between schools—they are contests between communities. These contests are one of the few events that pull people together in a group, one of the few chances they have for feeling and acting as a community. The old-time spelling bee is the only intellectual contest I know of that may have served a similar function. If it did, I suspect that spelling teachers were paid out of proportion to their fellow teachers, just as high school coaches are paid today out of proportion to other teachers.

One can certainly decry the high pay of football coaches and the low pay of science teachers. But the good science teacher is not performing the same function for the community as the winning coach. A winning team can give a whole community a good feeling about itself. Equally, a losing team can lower a community's self-esteem and make it look around for a coach who will restore its good feeling. So long as control of the schools is in the hands of the local community, or so long as there are no interscholastic contests into which the science teacher can send a team, the situation may be expected to persist.

A second problem among schools—one that holds back the school in the working-class suburb I mentioned earlier—may be summarized by the phrase "it's a long way from here to there." The students in this school have a long way to go, merely to catch up culturally with their contemporaries. When one stops to think, it is perhaps surprising that there is not more diversity among high schools than does exist, considering the diversity of cultural backgrounds with which they have to work.

The high school can be thought of as an intermediary between the community, on the one hand, and the demands of colleges or business and industry, on the other. As an intermediary, the school must meet the conditions at each end, and sometimes it is a long way between the two ends. This is why the school in the working-class suburb is happy to have athletes as popular heroes. Athletes, as opposed to hot-rodders and delinquents, represent a hard-won improvement in student ideals.

A similar problem exists when a school has diverse population needs to satisfy. The academically oriented, small town school to which I have referred several times has often been criticized by townspeople for paying too much attention to the children from the right side of the tracks, those who are going to college. Is this criticism justified? The question cannot be answered without first determining the most important function of the high school: is it to give college-bound students the knowledge and desire to learn that will carry them through college, or to train the noncollege students for their role in the community?

Another important explanation for the differences among high schools is the individual teachers in them. One teacher can have a remarkable influence on a school. There are five or six obvious examples in the schools we studied. One rather unfortunate case was that of the athletic director in the football-oriented school, whose effect was noted earlier. Another example I cited previously was the biology teacher whose class used five college texts. This teacher, whose fascination with biology was evident even in a short conversation, teaches in the school in the working-class suburb. His presence and his ability to intrigue students with the wonders of biology show how the long distance "from here to there" can sometimes be covered.

There are other instances: two excellent English teachers in the academically oriented small town school, an enthusiastic music teacher in one of the smaller schools, and others of their caliber have a great deal to do with the quality of education in the schools we studied. The fact that they can have such influence emphasizes the hunger that adolescents have for adult attention, and the response they give when adults show serious and continued interest in them.

Finally, let us turn to what may be the high school of the future—the plush suburban school with unlimited facilities. Does it really have a problem? A boy or girl *can* get an education there, and a very good one. (In many schools, he simply cannot; nor can he get a glimpse of the adventures possible in the world of the mind.) Furthermore, in this suburban school and others like it, the array of tempting educational morsels is laid out before the student within easy reach. Then what is the problem? Somehow, the average suburban student is not so hungry for these morsels. It is physically easy to feast on the morsels of learning set out for him, but it is psychologically hard. He wants to be part of the crowd, and the crowd is not having any. The crowd is interested in other things—dates, parties, sports, and the like. The suburban student may leave high school with all the learning he needs to provide him with a head start in college, but it is far from certain that he has the drive to use it to advantage.

Distractions from Learning

Why do such schools transmit knowledge without infusing a

desire for learning? This is a serious and difficult question to answer, and I shall attempt only a few speculations. Perhaps this is the fault of the students' fathers; they have succeeded too well. Their sons and daughters do not face the problem of how to get from here to there; the problem for them instead may be, "Where do we go from here?"

But this is too pat an answer. Even if it is part, it is not the whole answer. The suburban environment itself, and the concept of a school that encompasses the total social life of its students, may have something to do with it. It is often lamented that large city high schools cannot offer more extracurricular activities to their students, and that they cannot serve more of a community function. But this may be a fortunate failure. It may be that the very workaday atmosphere of these schools, lacking in multiple attractions and activities, helps the student to think of himself as a student, rather than as a teen-ager, by focusing his attention on the essential function of the high school—education.

Partly at fault, too, may be the notion that an excellent physical plant and teaching staff will necessarily capture the adolescent's imagination, regardless of the other bids for his or her attention in the community or in the school itself. There must be conscious and calculated attempts to capture students' imaginations with studies. Often this means introducing counterbalances in the system. For example, one element that needs counterbalancing in most large schools is something that seems almost trivial: that is, the importance of the girl cheerleader.

In many schools whose yearbooks we examined, it was evident that the cheerleaders were the popular idols for the girls. A girl is likely to expend more energy in trying to get on the cheerleading staff than she does on her studies. The importance given to the role of cheerleader seems in part to be related to the size of a school and the communication problems resulting from its size. What other girl has the chance to stand in front of the entire student body? What other girl in a school of two thousand students can be known to everyone?

Such "trivialities" as this are not trivial at all. They have little impact on what is taught, but they do divert the energies of students even further away from studies than they ordinarily tend to drift.

To summarize: I have tried first to show the differences in the substance of the education that high schools transmit. It is this difference to which we ordinarily refer when we speak of a high school's "quality." How much information has been furnished to its students? How well do they fare on standardized achievement tests? How many students enter advanced English or mathematics courses when they go to college? Using the criterion of substance, or quality of knowledge, there are differences among schools that are quite obvious. Some schools do not offer branches of learning that are common fare in others. Some schools make the knowledge they do offer very unappetizing; others impart information with a vigor that cannot fail to capture the students' interest.

Most of my attention in this discussion, however, has been devoted to a second difference among high schools. Less often recognized but, I submit, at least as important to a young person's future as the first, it is consequently at least as important in judging the quality of a high school. This is the general attitude toward education, toward scholastic achievement, and toward intellectual activity that prevails at a school. Does a boy come out of school aspiring to be a famous athlete or an esteemed scientist? Would he rather win the competition for girls or the prize for the best essay?

Such student attitudes are not the direct consequence of classroom experiences, but they are nevertheless the product of the school and the responsibility of the school. They stem from what might be called the "social organization" of the school, in contrast to its curriculum organization. This social organization has its values and norms; the standards are slanted either toward or away from intellectual endeavor.

For some reason, these matters of peer-group standards have never become part of an ideology or philosophy of education as have matters of curriculum content and style of teaching. This lack of attention may be due to the fact that these standards are not strictly related to the curriculum or to the style of teaching.

It is obvious, first of all, that the content of the curriculum is a responsibility of the school, and that it will affect the education a child receives. It is less obvious, but no less true, that the standards and values current among the students are primarily the responsibility of the school and do affect the education a child receives. The failure to incorporate an attention to student values in a formal philosophy of education means that each high school principal is on his own. If he is perceptive and imaginative and constantly alert, he can, along with his teachers, incline these peer-group standards toward educational goals. If the principal does not take interest or action, he leaves the molding of standards to the teen-agers themselves, as well as their absorption in those activities that happen to catch their attention.

Unfortunately, even if a principal is perceptive, imaginative, and alert, he may see this attention to student values as a kind of extraeducational task, not part of his core activities and decisions, which are focused around curriculum, staff, and physical plant. As a consequence, even in the best of high schools, these "climates of values" are left pretty much to develop on their own, with only such feeble intervention as the posting of the school's honor roll in the halls, whereas the school's athletes get their names and pictures spread all over the town newspaper.

3

Athletics in High School

The role of interscholastic athletics in high schools is a controversial one. Athletics is castigated as the antithesis of scholastic activity by intellectuals—many of whom have never taken part in interscholastic sports. It is defended and praised as the builder of men by coaches and athletes—most of whom have a vested interest in this proposition.

It is characteristic of athletics to provoke violent and lasting controversies, for it occupies a very special position in high schools. The amount of attention devoted to athletics would be most striking to an innocent visitor to a high school. A visitor entering a school would likely be confronted, first of all, with a trophy case. His examination of the trophies would reveal a curious fact: the gold and silver cups, with rare exception, symbolize victory in athletic contests, not scholastic ones. The figures adorning these trophies represent men passing footballs, shooting basketballs, holding out batons; they are not replicas of "The Thinker." The concrete symbols of victory are old footballs, basketballs, and baseballs, not works of art or first editions of books won as literary prizes. Altogether, the trophy case would suggest to the innocent visitor that he was entering an athletic club, not an educational institution.

Walking farther, this visitor would encounter teen-agers bursting from classrooms. Listening to their conversations, he would hear both casual and serious discussions of the Friday football game, confirming his initial impression. Attending a school assembly that morning, he would probably find a large segment of the program devoted to a practice of school cheers for the athletic game and the announcement of a pep rally before the game. At lunch hour, he would be likely to find more boys shooting baskets in the gymnasium than reading in the library. Browsing through a school yearbook, he would be impressed, in his innocence, with the number of pages devoted to athletics.

Altogether, this visitor would find, wherever he turned, a great deal of attention devoted to athletics. As an impressionable stranger, he might well suppose that more attention is paid to athletics by teen-agers, both as athletes and as spectators, than to scholastic matters. He might even conclude, with good reason, that the school was essentially organized around athletic contests and that scholastic matters were of lesser importance to all involved.

To be sure, his impression would vary from school to school —but, perhaps surprisingly, it would vary little by the social origins and destinations of the adolescents served by the schools. In the ten schools described in Chapter 2, athletics was about as dominant, by any of several criteria, in middle-class schools with a high proportion of graduates going to college as in working-class schools.[1]

Considering his impressions, such a visitor to American high schools might ask himself two questions: First of all, why is it this way? He had assumed, naively, that schools were for learning, yet his impressions led to a different conclusion. He had talked with educators about curriculum, new academic programs, and scholastic standards. Yet, upon visiting the schools, he found the adolescents' attention on athletics, and all the excitement and enthusiasm he found were focused around athletic contests. Why the discrepancy?

[1] See also James S. Coleman, *The Adolescent Society* (Glencoe: The Free Press, 1961), pp. 70–71, 88–90.

The visitor might ask another question: What are the consequences of the attention devoted to athletics? What are the consequences within the school itself, and what are the long-term consequences for these adolescents when they have become adults?

It is to these two questions, the question of consequences and the question of causes, that this chapter is directed. The examination will be based upon evidence collected during the study of the ten high schools previously discussed. Unless otherwise noted, the generalizations mentioned below apply to all the schools.[2] In fact, a striking discovery was the similarity of all the schools in the importance attached to athletics. Greater similarity among them was found in this than in any other dimension of the research.

Consequences

The more difficult question concerns the long-term consequences of attention to athletics. On this question, we have no concrete evidence, since adolescents were studied only during one year in high school, and there seem to be no systematic findings on the matter available elsewhere. However, evidence from the research does show some of the short-term consequences, those manifest in the school itself.

Impact on Freshmen

The attention focused upon athletics in high schools directly affects the impact of the schools on their incoming freshmen. Football, which is played in the fall as school begins, is especially important. A major element in the impact of athletics is the visibility of athletic stars. A boy who achieves something, however

[2] In certain cases, random variation owing to the small number of students in the smallest school prevents separate conclusions about it.

creditable, can be a model to emulate only if that achievement is exposed to view by the structure of activities in the school.

Some idea of the relative visibility of scholastic achievement and athletic achievement can be gained through a finding from the survey of the ten schools. About six weeks after school opened in the fall, each boy in every school was asked to name the boy whom he saw as the best student in his grade, and the boy who was the best athlete. This can be a difficult task for freshmen, but it is less difficult in those areas in which school activities focus attention on achievement. Thus, a comparison of the proportion of boys able to answer the questions provides some guide to the relative visibility of scholastic and athletic achievements in each of the four years of school.

Table 3–1 shows this comparison. The data indicate, in general, that the best athletes are more visible than the best scholars. The difference is greatest for the freshmen—the best athlete is known 10 per cent more often than the best scholar in the small schools, and 14 per cent more often in the large schools. Only in the junior and senior years does the visibility of the best scholars catch up with that of the best athletes. Thus, for the impressionable freshmen, the achievements that stand out most are those of the athlete, not those of the scholar.[3]

Assuming the adolescents' desire to be successful, known, and recognized, one consequence of the visibility of achievement in athletics or scholarship should be the desire to achieve in these particular areas. Does the environment and climate of opinion in the school affect these desires? Shortly after school had started in the fall, and again in the spring toward the end of the school year, boys were asked how they would most like to be remembered at school—as a brilliant student, an athletic star, or as most popular. One would suppose, if schools focus attention on scho-

[3] Other areas of achievement were included in the questionnaire, for example, knowing about cars and being most attractive to the girls. The visibility for both of these was far below that of athletes or scholars.

TABLE 3-1. Comparative Visibility of Best Athletes and Best Scholars among Their Classmates

	Freshmen	*Sophomores*	*Juniors*	*Seniors*
Small schools				
Per cent naming best athlete	68	75	88	85
Per cent naming best scholar	58	66	83	88
Number of cases	317	292	214	205
Large schools				
Per cent naming best athlete	54	56	48	72
Per cent naming best scholar	40	47	57	68
Number of cases	635	1,049	749	557

Note: Percentages are based on the nine public schools.

lastic endeavors, that the effect of the school year would be to increase the appeal of the brilliant student image relative to that of the athletic star image. Yet, for the freshmen and sophomores of the schools surveyed, matters were quite different. Of all those responding either "brilliant student" or "athletic star," 44 per cent in each grade responded "brilliant student" in the fall and only 37 per cent gave this response in the spring.[4] Rather than increasing in strength over the school year, the brilliant student image declined in appeal relative to that of the athlete. It appears, then, that the very functioning of the school itself tends to reduce the initial interest of the adolescent in being seen as a brilliant student, or tends to increase his interest in being seen as an athletic star.

Another effect of athletics on the incoming freshmen concerns the leading crowd in school. Most high schools, other than the very smallest, have a leading crowd in each grade; schools larger than about two thousand in enrollment may have more than one. This crowd is recognized by other students and by its own members, and most students can name members of the

[4] The number of cases was over eight hundred in each grade, so the difference reported is not due to chance variation.

leading crowd in their grade. This, in fact, was what they were asked to do in the research discussed above. In addition, all boys were asked to name their friends, so that it was possible to reconstruct the actual crowds or cliques in the school. Then, by identifying which cliques contained boys frequently named as members of the leading crowd, it was possible to identify objectively the leading clique or crowd in each grade of each school. Having done this, the question then was asked: What do these boys, who constitute the leading crowds in their grades, have in common?[5]

Among the freshmen in each of the four schools studied for leading cliques, the one attribute shared by every boy in every leading clique—twenty-three boys in all—was being out for either football or basketball. Most of the twenty-three were out for both. No other attribute—in background, activities, or attitudes—so sharply distinguished the leading cliques. In the later years of school, the leading cliques were found to be less uniformly athletic; but, among freshmen, they were found to be totally so.

Athletic participation as a basis for membership in the leading clique is not, of course, characteristic of every freshman class in the country; but it seems likely that the general tendency is widespread. Athletic teams provide a basis for intensive and prolonged association, more than any other activity in school. Thus, the foundation is laid, from the very beginning of high school, for a cohesive, tightly knit group. This, together with the attention directed toward athletic contests and athletic stars in high school, makes it very likely that the athletes will constitute the leading crowd among freshmen. Later, when other activities develop in school and groups form on other bases, there is less dominance by the athletic crowd. But, in the crucial first year, when a boy's aims and aspirations in high school are established, the athletic crowd dominates.

[5] This question was studied only in four of the five smallest schools; technical problems prevented it in the large schools, and the smallest school had no distinct crowds.

Altogether, then, athletics is a particularly important factor in the impact of the high school on its freshmen. Through the several mechanisms discussed above, the freshmen get a picture of the school focused even more on athletic achievement than it actually is.

Athletics in the Status System

One of the most important aspects of any social system is its distribution of status: the way status attaches to different persons and to different activities. The importance of the distribution of status lies partly in its effect as a motivating device, for it motivates people toward those activities that confer status on them. To the extent that adolescents are concerned with status among their peers—and every indication suggests that the great majority of them are so motivated—their motivations and aspirations in various activities are shaped by the distribution of status.

It is important, then, in assessing the consequences of the attention to athletics in high schools, to examine the position of athletics in the adolescent status system. In the research under discussion, this was done by several means.

Each boy was asked to assess what was required in his school to be a member of the leading crowd, and he was asked to rank various attributes for making a boy popular.

In response to the first question, the two attributes most often mentioned were personality—mentioned by 23 per cent of the boys—and a good reputation—mentioned by 17 per cent. Next in order, however, was athletic ability—mentioned by 16 per cent. This was followed by good looks and success with girls—mentioned by 14 per cent—and good grades or "brains"—mentioned by 12 per cent.

In ranking attributes for their effect in making a boy popular, six attributes were available to be ranked in order of importance, from first to sixth. These attributes, with their average rank in all schools, were the following:[6]

Being an athletic star	2.2
Being in the leading crowd	2.6
Leader in activities	2.9
High grades, honor roll	3.5
Having a nice car	3.9
Coming from the right family	4.5

These answers show the great value that boys attribute to athletic achievement in gaining popularity. It is ranked considerably above any other item and far above good grades, which is fourth among the six.

In addition to these subjective estimates, it is also possible to determine which boys have highest status. In this research, it was done by asking each boy to name another boy he would like to be like, one he would like to be friends with, and who were members of the leading crowd. The status of a boy was determined by the number of such choices he received. Another question had made it possible to identify the boys seen as the best athletes and the best scholars. By comparing the likelihood of the best athletes to receive the status choices with the likelihood of the best scholars to receive such choices, it is possible to examine the objective status of athletic achievement. Table 3–2 shows the average number of choices on these criteria received by the best athletes, the best scholars, and all other boys in the schools studied.

As in various other tests, athletics scored higher than scholarship, although both athletes and scholars far outdistanced other boys. To state the results another way, the star athletes, only 6.6 per cent of the schools' male enrollment, received 47.4 per

[6] The ranks average to 3.3 rather than 3.5 as they should, because not every boy assigned all ranks.

TABLE 3–2. Average Numbers of Choices Received by Athletes, Scholars, and All Other Boys on Status Criteria

	Be Friends with or Be Like	*Member of Leading Crowd*	*Number of Cases*
Athletes	5.6	7.8	272
Scholars	3.4	4.9	278
All other boys	0.4	0.8	3,598

Note: "Athletes" and "scholars" are those named two or more times as best athlete or best scholar in their respective grades by other boys. Percentages are based on the nine public schools.

cent of the "be friends with" and "be like" choices and 36.5 per cent of all the leading crowd nominations.

According to all evidence, then, the status of athletic achievement in the schools surveyed is exceedingly high, considerably higher than that of scholastic achievement. Thus, the attention paid to athletics in American high schools, which would so puzzle an innocent visitor, is paralleled by the status of athletic achievement among adolescents.

Other Studies

Other research shows that these facts are not limited to the ten schools surveyed or even to high schools in the Middle West.

In a large, predominantly Jewish, middle-class high school in New York City, Abraham Tannenbaum studied evaluations of stereotyped, fictitious students.[7] These fictitious students were described in short statements, in terms of intelligence, athletic ability, and studiousness. Juniors in the high school were then asked to ascribe traits—some desirable, some undesirable—to each of the eight fictitious characters. Tannenbaum devised a mean acceptability rating from the ascribed traits, and the ficti-

[7] Abraham J. Tannenbaum, "Adolescents' Attitudes toward Academic Brilliance" (unpublished doctoral dissertation, New York University, 1960).

tious students fell into the following order of acceptability, from high to low:

(1) Brilliant nonstudious athlete
(2) Average nonstudious athlete
(3) Average studious athlete
(4) Brilliant studious athlete
(5) Brilliant nonstudious nonathlete
(6) Average nonstudious nonathlete
(7) Average studious nonathlete
(8) Brilliant studious nonathlete.

As the order shows, all athletes had higher acceptability ratings than any nonathlete. Brilliance apparently had little effect in increasing acceptability, and studiousness reduced acceptability. Thus, in a school in which, because of its location and student body, one would expect to find brilliance or studiousness outdistancing athletics, the results are otherwise—and consistent with the results in the ten Midwestern high schools.

Athletics, Democracy, and Legitimacy of the System

The effect of athletics in forming leading crowds among freshman boys was examined earlier; the formation of leading crowds among girls was left unexamined. The cliques of girls among freshmen, much more than those of boys, reflect associations from earlier grades. Girls who travel together in the lower grades maintain their cliques in high school and often present an impregnable front to outsiders. Presumably as a result, the leading crowds for girls among freshmen are more completely middle class in background than for boys.

In effect, for boys athletics provides an interruption of this pattern, breaking down the organization based on common background and replacing it with one based on common activity or achievement. Perhaps as a consequence, boys are more willing than girls to accept the status system of the school and view it as more legitimate. When asked to agree or to disagree that "there are a few who control things in this school, and the rest of us are out in the cold," 43 per cent of the girls agreed with the statement in the fall, and the number increased to 48 per cent by the next spring. Only 34 per cent of the boys agreed that the statement was true in the fall, and their number decreased to 32 per cent by spring.

Such a democratizing mechanism is particularly important for boys, who, to begin with, are less involved in school than girls and get poorer grades. If it were not for interscholastic athletics or something like it, the rebellion against school, the rate of dropout, and the delinquency of boys might be far worse than they presently are. This can only be a matter of conjecture. It does seem clear, however, that athletics introduces an important democratizing factor in the status system for boys in high school by undercutting social background as a basis for status.

These multiple consequences of athletics in schools of widely varying types raise even more insistently the question of why there is such a dominance of athletics. Athletics is wholly outside the focus of attention of many educators in schools of education, for whom curriculum variations have overriding importance. Yet athletics is central to the attention of adolescents, far more so than curriculum variations. And, despite educators' professional disinterest, athletics is an activity promoted by the schools themselves—not an outside interest like cars and dates. These inconsistencies and paradoxes all lead to the question: Why does athletics hold a place of such high importance in the high schools?

Causes

Clearly, a part of the importance of athletics for adolescents lies in its compatibility with teen-age energy, enthusiasm, and explosive spirits. Were it not for this basic compatibility, the avidity with which teen-agers follow sports contests would be difficult to explain.

But the compatibility does not explain the special place that athletics holds in the activities of a school. As an innocent visitor might observe, the institution itself often seems more oriented toward athletic goals than academic ones. This can hardly be explained by the interests of teen-agers alone, for teen-agers are interested in many things—popular music, cars, dates—that have relatively little place in the high school structure of activities. Nor can the interests of teen-agers explain the fact that, in the ten schools surveyed, the appeal of the athletic-star image increased during the school year and, apparently, decreased over the summer.[8]

Athletic contests in schools seem to serve an important function for the institution. Every institution depends for its survival upon capturing a certain portion of the energies of its members. In business organizations, this is done by pay, including incentive pay, and by opportunity for promotion. Among some members of an organization, identification with the achievements of the organization provides additional motivation. In unions, motivation derives from the common goals of the members, which can only be gained through concerted, collective effort.[9]

Schools, however, provide no comparable motivating devices for their students. Students are forced by family and by law to attend school, but this ensures only their physical presence, not their involvement in school activities. The necessary motivation for the expenditure of effort in school arises naturally only for those students whose backgrounds and aspirations make good grades important for them. For some students, that is, grades are comparable to pay for workers in a factory. The

[8] For further discussion of this point, see Coleman, *op. cit.*, p. 303.

[9] When a union becomes merely a business union, no longer actively fighting for collective worker benefits, it survives in name, but it can no longer depend upon its members for active support. This, in fact, is the fundamental problem of many unions at the present time.

crucial difference is that grades are important only for a part of the school population and that good grades can be obtained by only a part of the school population. For many adolescents, high school only delays their access to adult freedoms and pleasures and does not offer any unique and necessary benefits.

But, even for students with the right backgrounds, grades are a poor motivating mechanism, because they are unique to the school and useful only in comparison with grades of fellow students. This generates invidious comparisons, sets each student in competition with his fellows, and is a powerfully divisive force among the students. Direct incentive pay, or piece work, in factories produces the same effect and has sometimes been consciously used by employers to keep employees divided against each other.[10]

In the long run, this is a dangerous mechanism, as the history of incentive pay has shown. Under many conditions, it encourages informal norms restricting production—against the "rate-buster"—just as grade systems in high schools promote informal action against too much studiousness—against "the curve-raiser" or the "D.A.R.," damned average raiser. Finally, piece work systems in factories have led to organized collective activity against the companies, unless the workers feel strongly identified with their companies.[11]

A much more successful mechanism of control in an institu-

[10] This can be illustrated by the story, perhaps apocryphal, of the employer who paid every second worker on an assembly line a higher rate, so that every worker's neighbors received rates different from his own. A similar mechanism has been documented in department stores, where clerks are given marginal differentiations in title and pay to keep them divided. See Carl Dreyfuss, "Prestige Grading: A Mechanism of Control," in R. K. Merton and others, *Reader in Bureaucracy* (Glencoe: The Free Press, 1952), pp. 258–264.

[11] One of the important reasons that incentive pay, in the form of commissions, has always worked well for salesmen is that their active work in selling the company products to doubtful customers generates in them a positive identification with the company. Another reason, of course, is that they are usually dispersed, not in contact with one another.

tion is one that generates strong positive identification with the institution. Churches employ such mechanisms with their revival meetings and special holy day services. Associations and groups of all sorts do the same with rallies and collective events. But schools—apart from their athletic contests and similar activities—are peculiar institutions. There are no collective goals that the students share, and the institution is lifeless. There are only individual goals, individual scholastic achievements, made largely at the expense of other students.

Athletic contests with other schools provide, for these otherwise lifeless institutions, the collective goals that they lack. The common goals shared by all make the institution part of its members and them part of it, rather than an organization outside them and superimposed upon them. The results are evident to any observer: The adolescent social system is centered at the school, not at the drugstore; the name by which the teen-agers identify themselves is that of the school ("Those are East High kids; I'm from Tech."); the teen-agers think of the school, the team, and the student body as one and use the pronoun "we" in referring to this entity ("We're playing Parkville Friday.").

Such effects are evident as well in the bases of alumni loyalty to many private preparatory schools and colleges. Athletic competition as a basis of loyalty is so dominant that the stereotypical alumnus is a man cheering wildly at a football game, waving a school banner in his hand. Colleges that dropped interscholastic athletics, like the University of Chicago, or that never depended on them, like Johns Hopkins, thereby sacrificed the attention and support of many alumni.[12] Historians have noted that col-

[12] This is not to say that the absence of athletic emphasis in these institutions has principally bad consequences. Rather, many colleges have compromised their original goals through the power and interest of their athletically involved alumni. But the withdrawal from interscholastic athletics without the substitution of other bases for institution-inspired pride and identification leaves the institution weaker and less likely to survive.

leges in the United States, before the introduction of organized sports, were beset by student violence directed at both the college and other students. Sports seemed to transform the disorganized and explosive student body into a close-knit community with strong common goals.

Thus, the importance of athletic contests in both high schools and colleges lies, at least in part, in the way the contests solve a difficult problem for the institution—the problem of generating enthusiasm for and identification with the school and of drawing the energies of adolescents into the school.

In the study of the ten high schools on which much of this chapter is based, all students were asked, "If school were not compulsory and it were completely up to you, would you stay in school until graduation, leave school before graduation, or are you undecided?" Very few students, only 3.6 per cent, responded that they would leave, and only 9.3 per cent were undecided. It is hard to imagine that the great number of adolescents in our society who have been brought into high school in such a short period could be so positively oriented to school without some mechanism such as athletic contests for providing common goals.[13]

Lack of Common Community Goals

A force that strengthens the emphasis on athletics in the high schools comes from outside the schools themselves. Except in the very largest cities, a high school is a community or neighborhood institution. Many communities have only a single high school, whose name is the name of the town. In those cities with several high schools, each school usually represents a community area within the city and often carries the name of that community.

[13] This suggests that high schools in Europe, which are coming to enroll larger and larger proportions of adolescents, will increase the emphasis upon athletic contests, unless they find another mechanism to accomplish the same end.

Communities, like schools without interscholastic games, have few common goals. They fight no wars, seldom engage in community rallies, and are rarely faced with such crises as floods or tornadoes that can engender a communal spirit and make members feel close to one another by creating collective goals. One of the few mechanisms by means of which this can occur is that of games or contests between communities. Sometimes these games are between professional teams representing the communities.[14] More often, they are high school games, and these contests serve the purpose admirably. The community supports the team, and the team rewards the community when it wins. The team is a community enterprise; its successes are shared by the community, and its losses mourned in concert.

The results of this are evident in many ways. One striking evidence is teacher salaries. The school board characteristically pays more to athletic coaches than to other teachers and, occasionally, to keep a winning coach, may pay more to him than to the principal. When a new principal is to be found among the ranks of teachers, the pattern is common for the athletic coach to be promoted to the job.

Another indicator is buildings. It is often easier to obtain funds for a new gymnasium—especially in "basketball territory"—than for other buildings. In Paris, Illinois, for example, where the high school team had won the state basketball tournament, the community voted funds for a large new gymnasium, while the high school remained without a library. In one of the ten schools included in the survey, the author found, on returning at a later date, that a new gymnasium and a new reading room had been built. Funds for the gymnasium had been donated by a member of the community; the reading room had been added by means of school building funds.

[14] The sense of shock and disbelief in Brooklyn when the Dodgers moved to Los Angeles is a measure of Brooklynites' identification of the team with their community. On the other hand, it has been said that Los Angeles ceased to be a collection of suburbs and became a city for the first time when "their" Dodgers won a pennant.

Altogether, it is clear that the causes of attention to athletics in a high school are basic to the functioning of the school itself. Athletics fills a serious vacuum, in establishing collective goals for the school and community; if some of this attention is to be focused on educational activities, they too must contribute toward those collective goals.

4

The Economy and Secondary Education

It is no longer possible to make an easy connection between general prosperity and the abundance of jobs. Several things have combined to break this connection. First, we have learned to manufacture goods without the aid of the physical labor of men; we call it automation, but whatever its name, it is rapidly cutting away the entire bottom segment of the job market. Second, in 1945, we sharply increased our manufacture of babies; they are now moving into the labor market. Third, though we know how to manufacture babies at a rapid rate, we have not learned how to transform a majority of them into adults who can perform *mental* rather than *physical* labor for hire.

A few statistics will reveal the problem better than words.[1] Figure 4–1 shows nonagricultural occupations ordered according to the average education of those in the occupation, as well as the 1962 unemployment rate in each occupation. The economy has less use for the occupations at the lower education end of the occupational scale. Those who have entered at the low end now find themselves likely to be without a job; those who

[1] Statistics used in compiling figures 4–2 and 4–4 are taken from U.S. Dept. of Labor, *Manpower and Training* (Washington: Government Printing Office, Feb. 5, 1963). I am grateful also to Daniel P. Moynihan, Assistant Secretary of Labor, for aid in providing statistical materials used in this chapter.

have entered at the high end find themselves more and more in demand, able to command higher and higher salaries.

As to our manufacture of more babies, Figure 4–2 shows the changes in the 14–24 age segment of the labor force between the 1950–1960 period and the projected change in the 1960–1970 period:

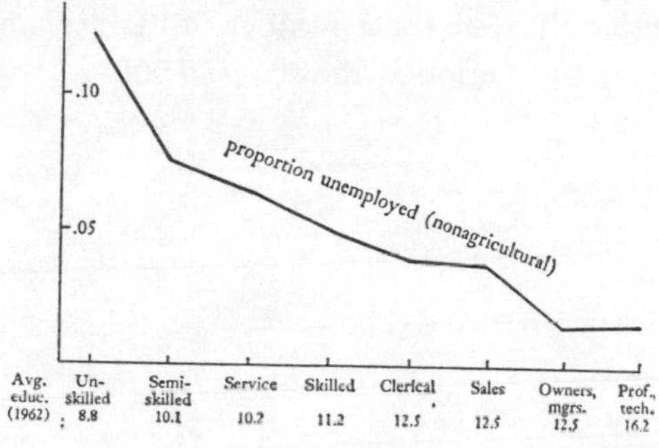

Figure 4–1

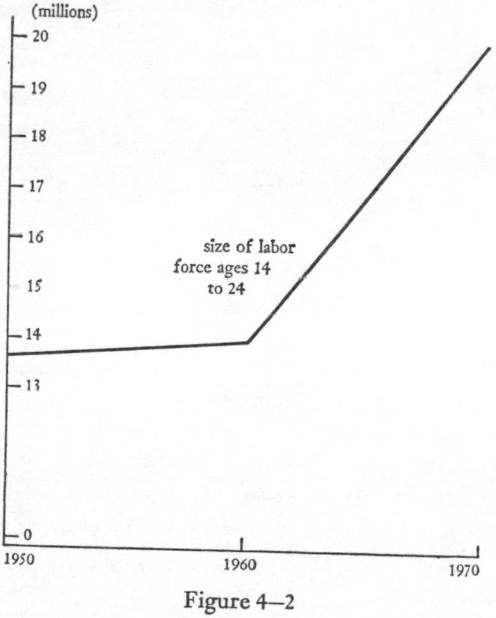

(millions)
20
19
18
17
16
15
14
13
0
size of labor force ages 14 to 24
1950
1960
1970

Figure 4–2

Finally, Figure 4–3 shows the projected proportion of high-school students who will drop out between 1960 and 1970 (based on the change in rate of dropouts that occurred between 1960 and 1962). As the chart indicates, the expected reduction in proportion of dropouts is extremely small, and, of course, because of the high birth rates, the absolute number of dropouts will increase sharply. The total number of high school dropouts expected during this period is about 7,300,000.

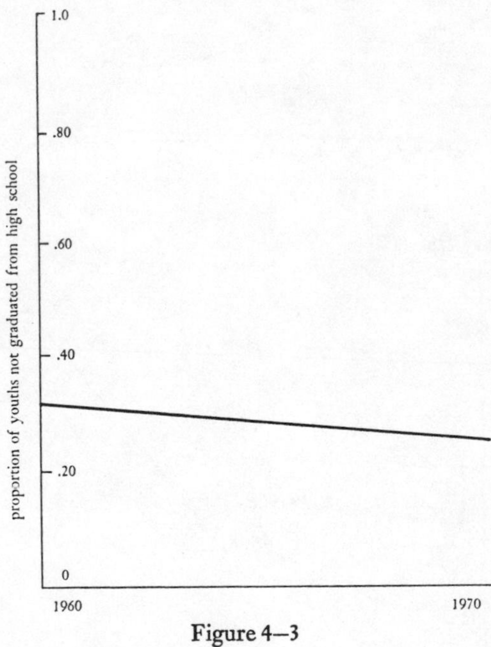

Figure 4–3

The magnitude of the problem can be shown in a different way. If we project the increase in number of jobs in society (based on trends between 1957 and 1962) and the increase in number of persons to fill those jobs, we obtain the picture shown in Figure 4–4.

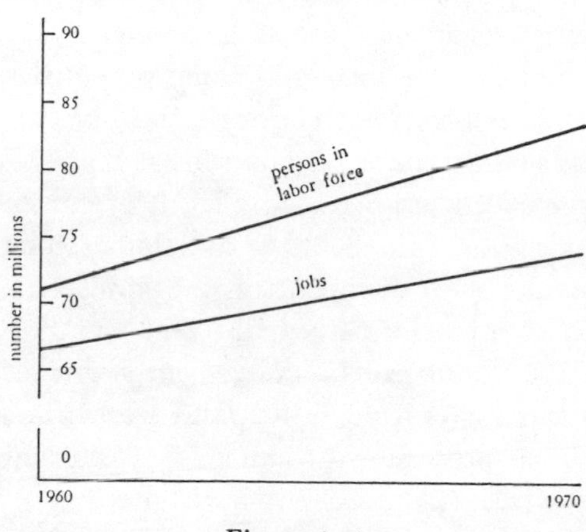

Figure 4–4

The number of jobs is increasing at a snail's pace, about 550,000 per year, whereas the size of the labor force is increasing at about 1,300,000 per year. This means a vast number of new unemployed by 1970 to add to the present 4,000,000. The relative rates of unemployment in the sixteen to twenty-four and and the twenty-five-plus age groups are now about 11 per cent to 4 per cent. If these rates maintain their same relation, about 22 per cent of the young (sixteen to twenty-four, not in school) will be unemployed, and about 8 per cent of those twenty-five and older. (Even now in 1965, the unemployment rate among Negro youth is about 27 per cent.)

The sharp increase in the birth rate in 1946 and beyond requires us to take a closer look at the problems it creates. It is important to recognize that the increase in youth reaching employment age exists at all levels of education, not merely at the lowest educational levels, such as the high school dropouts. Therefore, there will have to be adjustments in institutions to cope with the increase at all levels rather than merely at the lowest level. This is important to recognize, because often we take a simplified view, looking only at the most difficult problem such as that which exists at the lowest educational levels. To do so, however, means that we may miss some potential solutions to the problems, because some solutions could involve an interaction of sorts between the excess persons at high levels of education and the excess persons at low levels of education.

Putting aside for the moment the question of such policy solutions, I want first to comment on the kinds of institutional adjustments that are occurring at different levels of education. To do this, the youth can be conveniently divided into four groups: (1) those who have in the past entered the labor force after graduate or professional training, that is, training beyond a bachelor's degree; (2) those who have entered the labor force directly after a college degree or, at least, some years of college; (3) those who have entered the labor force directly after high school, perhaps supplemented by specific business or technical courses; and (4) those who have entered the labor force before completion of high school, often termed high school dropouts. My comments will concern what are the present and emerging patterns among each of these groups.

(1) Among the segment who, during the 1950's, would have gone to graduate or professional school, there is no change in pattern. Today they are taking graduate or professional training and will enter labor markets where the demand for their services is high.

(2) Among those who would have entered the labor market after college, there is a massive change in progress. Instead of entering the labor force directly, many are continuing in school to obtain graduate or professional training. This is in considerable part a response to the type of new job formation which characterizes the present. There is little new job formation in the private sector of the economy. The new job formation in the public and nonprofit sector is largely in professional and technical occupations. Thus, the position in business that was

open to the college graduate without specific technical or professional training is far less frequent. A college graduate, surveying the job possibilities, finds few such jobs but many jobs awaiting those who have additional training ranging all the way from a master's degree in social work to an M. D. There are exceptions, of course, in which a college degree provides specific technical or professional training. The two most important are engineering and teaching. Jobs for college graduates in these fields continue to be available enough so that this massive movement from college into graduate training is less evident.

One point that is important to note, since it will contrast with other educational levels, is that there is no real barrier to such movement, except for the rather flexible one of size of graduate training facilities. Though this constitutes some barrier as the 1946 babies graduate from college, there is no ability or background barrier. This results from the fact that the intellectual hurdle of graduate training is no higher than that of college; therefore, those who have graduated from college have sufficient ability to be successful in some type of graduate study.

(3) Among those who would have entered the labor force directly after high school, there is similarly a change, though not as complete as among the college graduates. This change is toward entry into college of some sort. Junior college is the most evident pattern; another is the new four-year community college. The development of these new institutions occurs at a level of intellectual requirement appropriate for high school graduates who in former years would not have gone to college. Consequently, as in the college-graduate school transition, there is not a serious differential in the intellectual hurdle required.

However, there is a large segment of high school graduates who are not making this shift, yet for whom there are no jobs in the labor force. Partly the barrier is financial; partly it is intellectual. (I use the term "intellectual" here to cover a multitude of things not easily separated, ranging all the way from intellectual ability to the willingness to sit passively in a classroom in the role of student.) Though neither of these barriers exists for some proportion of high school graduates who have not in the past gone to college (thus making junior college a reasonable solution for them), one or the other does exist for a large number of others. Therefore, at this level there is coming to be a serious problem of large numbers of youth with nowhere to go–neither to further education, for the reasons above, nor to a job, for the job does not exist.

(4) Among those who would have entered the labor force without completing high school, there is very little change. That is, the rate of retention in high school is increasing only very slowly; thus very few of the youth who, in the 1950's, would not have finished high school are presently finishing high school. The reason for this appears to be the nature of our educational system, together with chronic background or family deficiencies of somewhere between a fourth and a third of youth. (This differs extremely in different parts of the country, being between zero and 5 per cent in such states as Minnesota and Oregon, but very high in some southern states and large cities.) Given the family deficiencies that exist for a large part of the Negro population and a segment of the white population most highly represented in the rural South, present educational systems are not able to hold these segments–even when the alternative for the young person is unemployment or underemployment. Because of this powerful barrier, the possibility of these youths continuing in school is very small. As a result, they are dumped on the labor market. Along with the segment of high school graduates for whom there is an intellectual or financial barrier to junior college, these people constitute the most visible problem; for there are neither educational institutions nor jobs that can absorb them.

This, then, constitutes the present state as I see it. There are a number of possible paths to solutions to the problems created. One major path is that of stimulating the rate of new job creation, thus increasing the demand in those sectors of the labor market where there is oversupply. The "blind" or nonanalytical approach to this is simply a general stimulation of the economy, with a hope that the new jobs that open up will not fall at educational levels 1 or 2 (where there will be no problem because of existing strong demands at level 1 and the ability of graduate training to absorb those at level 2), but will fall instead at levels 3 and 4. The tax cut of 1964 was in part designed for this purpose and is expected to have this effect by a large and respectable body of economists. In my opinion, they could not be more incorrect. The tax cut will have little effect where the problems are greatest. Instead, the affluent segment of the society will become more affluent, and the competitively disabled (at levels 3 and 4) will remain dependent.

The defects in the analysis behind such proposals to generally stimulate the economy may be seen by use of an equation relating work input and productivity output:

production/man-hour × men in labor force × hours/week × employment rate = amount of production per week

This equation is often loosely used to imply cause and effect. It is often assumed that, if we merely find a way to increase economic growth (that is, make the demand for production grow faster), then this will reduce unemployment. And to be sure, if everything in the above equation is held constant except the employment rate and if production is boosted, then, of course, the employment rate must increase.

The fallacy lies in assuming that there is a single equation, a single labor market in our economy. Thus, although there is over-all high unemployment, in professional and technical occupations there is little. Thus, an increase in the product from industries in this sector (e.g., space, scientific research) means only that the production per man-hour or the hours per week has increased.

There are only two ways that infusion of more money into

a sector of the economy can affect unemployment: either by increasing the employment rate in that sector or by drawing more men into that sector from others where the employment rate is low, i.e., by increasing the second factor or the fourth factor in the above equation. In short, the money must go into those sectors of the labor market where unemployed youths find themselves (factor 4) or into allied sectors to which they can easily move (factor 2).

This is where much of the problem lies. For the unemployed youth are by no means a random sample; they include many school dropouts and are unskilled or semiskilled, trained only for general blue-collar labor or the most intellectually undemanding of white-collar labor. There are many forces that are combining to move money out of these sectors (or to increase the production per man-hour while holding total production constant, which has the same effect). Automation is shifting whole industries out of these sectors. A prime example is the chemical industry, where production now requires skilled attendants for control systems and has decreasing use for semiskilled laborers. Another example is the more efficient methods of marketing, as in discount stores and supermarkets, which have much larger sales volume per employee than a few years ago. Thus retail-store clerking, for long an important source of jobs for youth, is less abundant.

Furthermore, the current "natural" economic growth is in areas at the opposite end of the labor market from the unemployed youth—in scientific research, engineering, space exploration, missile development, and defense production of a highly technical sort. Even natural economic growth from consumer goods will do little for the unemployed youth, for a larger and larger proportion of consumer goods is produced and sold without the aid of unskilled or semiskilled.

In fact, it appears that the causation is in the opposite direction; economic growth is being kept down by the lack of persons in the right parts of the labor force, i.e., in the most highly trained sectors. For example, Congress has been ready to appropriate more money than requested for space exploration and has been prevented only by testimony from agency officials that the added money will not help because the additional people with the right abilities are not available. As another example, the salaries of university professors continue to rise, wholly because of market conditions, there are not enough to go around. Similarly, there is money for more people in medical research, in research on juvenile delinquency, and in research for science generally. Our speed in getting a man on the moon or in getting a cancer cure is not limited by the money invested in these areas; it is limited by the relatively small numbers of people able to work in them.

One consequence of this is that salaries are artificially high for scientists, doctors, college teachers, and other professionals. The inadequacies of the educational system have artificially restricted the supply of such people.

This discussion suggests that to look toward a high rate of economic growth as a solution puts the cause where the effect should be; natural economic growth will result if we get more men into the high-demand segments of the labor market. These high-demand segments are at the high-education end of the labor market, where most of the unemployed youth can never get. In economists' terms, the elasticity of this segment of the labor market is quite low. In human terms, if a boy doesn't get a good education early in life, many paths are blocked to him. It should be noted that the principal point of difference between my analysis and that of those who argue that mere economic growth will solve the problem lies at this point. Those persons argue that it is relatively easy to move from one sector of the labor force to another when demand is high, that a man may be trained by a firm for new skills. As indicated above in the analysis of educational changes among four groups of youth, this is probably more nearly true at higher levels than at lower ones.

There might, however, be somewhat more sophisticated stimulation to create new jobs in the right places. This could be called "selective stimulation" of the economy. It would not occur through a tax cut but through government contracts for various public works.

Another possible way of stimulating new job creation at these levels is a reduction of the work week. This would probably not have much direct effect. For example, even though basic work weeks in skilled crafts decrease and unemployment increases, the actual work week of employed workers in these skills remains stable—and high—from forty-two to forty-four hours per week, depending on the craft. Overtime for various reasons usually is more efficient than the hiring of extra workers. Also, any reduction in the work week will increase the number of men among the competitively advantaged who hold two jobs. Thus it is conceivable that such reduction would actually increase unemployment. However, some manpower economists whose opinion I respect, in particular Eli Ginsberg, propose that the indirect effects would be great, opening up new industries to cater to the increased leisure and thus new jobs.

There are possible means of increasing the demand for youth other than by stimulating the private economy. One means is by explicit creation of new jobs in the public sector. The Peace Corps is one example. Another would be the development of a large urban recreational program for children. This would create many jobs for recreational leaders. There is a wide array of such possibilities, including many of those explored during the WPA.

The other major path to a solution concerns reduction of supply of these youth, or shifting the supply to different sectors of the economy. One method of shifting the supply, in present use, is through job-training programs. This approach has certain merits, for it can move the youth from areas of heavy oversupply of labor to areas with only medium oversupply. But short-term job-training programs can hardly do more than that. These programs begin too late and end too soon; as a consequence, their aid is minor. To be specific, present job-training programs focus on the wrong occupations. Nearly two-thirds of those in training are preparing for blue-collar jobs, where unemployment is presently great and jobs are increasing very slowly. This solution consequently is only a stopgap for the young, for it trains for occupations where jobs will be relatively scarcer each year.

The job-training programs necessary if the problem is to be solved are of a much more radical sort. A program such as the Job Corps, which combines training with work, is one important example. Another example is an interesting experiment in Chicago that the Encyclopedia Britannica company has conducted: an experimental evening high school principally for school dropouts using advanced teaching techniques and getting high performance out of the once rebellious students.

Suppose the federal, state, or city government were to invest in such educational entrepreneurs in cities throughout the country—educational entrepreneurs who would take the culls of the system and teach to get results (not, as in many public schools at present, merely to maintain discipline). If paid according to results, with students tested by government examiners, I suspect that capitalist enterprise would produce some remarkable successes. The government, in turn, would not be spending its money unwisely but would be investing in a profit-making enterprise, since every success would mean removing a person from a status of dependence on society and allowing him to move into a high-demand sector of the economy where he would pay back in taxes and in contributions to economic growth many times the money invested in him in his youth.

Another means of reducing the supply of untrained youth is the obvious one of keeping more people in school longer. In the long run, some such solution as this is necessary. Yet the short-run outlook is dim indeed. Between 1960 and 1962, the high school dropout rate decreased only from 31.5 per cent to 30.3 per cent.

In the schools from which the unemployed youth come, the teachers are often little more than disciplinarians; the school considers itself successful if it is merely able to maintain order and keep students in school. As a consequence, the high school diploma is little more than recognition that the boy or girl will keep quiet and obey orders. In Washington, D.C., where the problem is particularly acute, the superintendent of schools is quoted as follows in an interview:[2]

Q. Under your system is it possible for a student to get a high school diploma without being able to read and write?

A. No. I did not say that a pupil would be graduated without ability to read and write. I said that, in the basic track, some of the slower ones might be reading at the sixth-grade level, which is a functional level.

Q. A high-school education used to mean, at least, that you could read and write. . . .

A. I hope it still does.

One proposal that has been made is to increase the age of compulsory school attendance. This, I believe, is a totally incorrect approach. It is important to make this clear because a number of influential persons are beginning to advocate it. The present school dropouts are extremely difficult to retain in school given our present teaching methods. If they were to be forced to remain for another year or two, the problems of school rebellion and delinquent activities would increase enormously. The hard core of students who presently do not finish would not emerge from school any better prepared for the labor force. They simply would have been in custody for one or two years and, released from custody, be less fit for the labor force than a boy

[2] *U.S. News & World Report*, March 11, 1963.

who presently leaves school at sixteen, just as a boy who is forced to remain in school until sixteen today may be less fit for the labor force than his counterpart who left at age fourteen a generation or two ago.

Radical changes in the whole structure of secondary education are necessary if the situation is to be modified. A major difficulty with the present system is that it tends to be monolithic. Allowing an adolescent greater freedom in choosing his training (thereby placing more responsibility on him for completing it) and giving him the chance to move from one school to another (but with the possibility of being "fired," just as from a job) rather than compelling him to go every day to a school he did not choose, to a teacher he does not like, or to do things he considers childish would go a long way toward giving the adolescent a stake in his own future and thus win his active support.

The federal government's aid to education should do more than merely strengthen the present public school system. For example, the federal government could establish free supplementary schools of various kinds, using innovations that would be impossible and in fact undesirable to introduce into the total school system. Such schools could be attended part of the day on a voluntary basis through a released-time arrangement with the city's public schools.

Other proposals in this direction could also get at the root of the problem. The difficulty for the group at educational level 4 and part of those at level 3 (the high school dropouts and those who barely finish) is the combination of school as presently constituted, and family background. By taking these adolescents into such a program as military service or the CCC or Job Corps, they can be taught. Experience, particularly in the military, has shown that well. Thus, certain kinds of program that would involve the young person's leaving his current environment and going into some form of living–school–work arrangement might be extremely effective. First, it would prepare these youths for certain jobs they cannot now hold; second, it would remove the barrier to further education (either part-time or full-time); third, it would give them some experience in responsible work activity, which is one valuable element in the ability to be successful in the labor force; and, fourth, it would provide a temporary decrease in the supply of unskilled youth.

Another strategy is being carried out in Canada. Because technical jobs are in relatively good supply, the increase in post–high school education there is taking the form of government-sponsored and stimulated technical institutes. These provide a training period of two or three years; but they give technical training at reasonably high levels of skill, and, as a consequence, they are probably far more useful to their students than a regular junior college.

These are only a few of numerous possibilities; as the educational entrepreneurs mentioned earlier, doing "job-training" wholly for white-collar occupations, is another. There exists a whole range of possibilities for making the educational system less monolithic and for educating a higher proportion of the young. In addition to these changes, we need to develop a concept of "real education" (analogous to "real income") measured in terms of its value in the labor market.

Where do all these proposals and possibilities leave us? Several points seem clear:

(1) With the present rates of increase in labor supply and job supply, there will be more and more unemployed (over 10,000,000 in seven years, compared to 4,000,000 now). Over half of them will be under twenty-five years of age.

(2) The growth rate of the economy is being hindered by the lack of highly educated persons. If the educational system were functioning properly, the supply of highly educated would match the high demand; salaries in that sector would decline to more normal levels, and the number of jobs would increase; pro-

ductivity (particularly of innovations, which set in motion further productivity) would increase; and the labor pressure would move off the oversupplied occupations.

(3) Economic growth is also hindered by the failure to match increases in consumer expenditures with increases in public expenditures. Thus, as Galbraith points out, there is a relative starvation of the public sector of the economy—simply because certain expenditures, such as those for public-recreation areas, schools, mass transit, etc., must be made as collective (i.e., political) decisions rather than individual ones. We have not developed institutions that allow us to make those decisions as readily as we make individual consumer decisions.

Two kinds of action then are called for in order to avert a national disaster. The first is immediate and large-scale attention to the educational system, for here lies the greatest present barrier to an expanding economy with high employment. Such attention should probably bypass the politically difficult hurdles of aid to state and local school systems; but it should provide other alternatives that can pull a boy or girl out of the plight the present system has put him in and, at the same time, relieve the pressure on the public schools. The efforts should not be restricted to the high school level; the economy's strong demand is for persons with further training. At the college level, the problem is principally a financial one. (Research that I carried out on the question of college choice suggests that lack of finances was the principal element in a bright boy's or girl's failure to consider a college beyond the local teachers college.) A very large-scale college scholarship program would overcome the principal barrier at this level. It is important, of course, that these programs at the high school and college levels be instituted quickly, for the babies of the post-war years are coming of age.

The second type of action is high and continuous expenditures on public works. There are, it should be recognized, two opposite forms of public expenditures in terms of their effect on unemployment. The first is outside the country, as foreign aid, or in high-employment areas of the economy: defense expenditures, space research and development, medical research, scientific research, etc. This probably increases unemployment, at least in the short run, by taking money from sectors of medium employment (through taxes) into sectors of high employment. The other is in sectors of low employment, utilizing low-skilled labor. Many public works are of this latter sort: construction of all kinds, forestry and conservation, child care, recreational supervision. It is this latter form of public expenditure that can have a short-term impact on unemployment in all age groups.

But Congress has difficulty passing adequate legislation even with the facts so clear. Why is this? The answer apparently lies in two areas. First, the problem is only beginning to increase in magnitude. Its major impact lies in the future—albeit the very near future. Our government, and in particular Congress, with its finger on the pulse of national sentiments, tends to react to the problems of today. As long as problems changed slowly, as they did in the past, such reactive legislation worked reasonably well. But today the ever faster changes in technology and the violent swings in the birth rate create problems that arise so rapidly as to make such government-by-popular-reaction hardly equal to the task.

The second reason is that, for the first time, the Gross National Product has contained to move upward, while unemployment has swelled. This means—as numerous essayists[3] have pointed out—that two segments of our economy are going in opposite directions. As a consequence, while a minority of each Congressman's constituents is worse off than ever before, the majority is better off and sees no problems. Thus there is no national urgency, no willingness to establish large-scale public-works programs. It is

[3] See, e.g., Michael Harrington, *The Other America: Poverty in the United States* (New York: Macmillan, 1962).

paradoxical that in the 1930's, when there were fewer unemployed youth than there will be in 1966 and when our economy could ill afford it, Congress was willing to vote massive public works and a CCC, yet today it provides only small "pilot" programs.

Concluding Remarks on Real Education

In some respects, the perspective of this chapter appears sharply different from the perspective taken in chapters 2 and 3 and that to be taken in chapters 5 and 6. It deals with numbers, with the question of how many persons are processed through what stages of formal education. It treats quantity, whereas the other chapters treat quality of education. This perspective may convey the illusion that the essential question is how many persons pass through particular stages of formal education and not what they learn in those stages. Indeed, this is the view taken by some employers, who appear more concerned with a high school diploma, a B.A., or a Ph.D. than with the qualifications of a job applicant.

But clearly, however much these pieces of paper may help an individual to get a job, they are of no value for the functioning of the society or the economy. What is important, of course, is the kind of transformation that a man has undergone to make him a valuable member of society. Thus, even in the quantitative study of education, as carried out in this chapter, the crucial question is quality. As indicated in this chapter, what is necessary is some concept of *real education*, so that when the quality of a high school diploma goes down as the quantity goes up, we will not be misled into believing that something has been gained.

But the concept of real education can have two quite different meanings. One is provided by academic measuring sticks, which show the achievement levels reached in various subjects. The wide variety of standardized tests used in schools provide such measuring sticks, measures that are widely used for entrance to college and to graduate study.

A quite different concept of real education lies in a direct analogue with real income: what value it has in obtaining other things. For this, the appropriate measure of real education is just what it will do for the owner: what kind of a job it will get him and how it will aid him in advancement and achievement in that job, how it will help him to pursue a satisfying life. Part of this, its aid in getting him a job, is directly measurable, although other parts are far more difficult to measure. But let us assume for a moment that it was wholly measurable and that we could obtain a measure of real education in terms of what it would do for the individual throughout life.

Unfortunately, neither of these measures is quite right. The academic measures do provide absolute standards of achievement, but this achievement may be totally irrelevant to the individual's future activities. Schools are well known to focus their energies on teaching irrelevancies; and even if certain skills (e.g., reading knowledge of Latin) are not wholly irrelevant, how are they to be weighted? The same can be said even for subjects which obviously have relevance: ability to calculate, knowledge of consumer economics, or skill in English composition.

Clearly the value of the education cannot be measured this way, but neither does it lie in the other measure. For we are interested in the intrinsic value of education for society and the economy. The market value of a high school or college diploma is no measure of this. As a simple illustration, such market value will fluctuate with short-term variations in the economy; yet the value to society of an engineer graduated in 1949, during a mild recession, and one graduated two years later, during a period of prosperity, is alike, even though their diplomas have different market values. As another example, if employers do react to the formal degree itself rather than to the quality of knowledge and ability, then the formal degree has market value along with the knowledge and ability. Yet it is the knowledge and ability that benefits society and the holder of the degree in the long run.

In some respects, the quality that more than anything else approaches what is required in the concept of real education is self-responsibility. If a person can take care of himself, can be both economically and socially independent, then he has the necessities for living. If he can do so in a wide variety of circumstances, then he has a higher level of real education. If, for example, he can retrain himself for a job or can maintain his psychological equilibrium in solitary confinement, then he has a high level of what he needs for living. Even in advanced professional and scientific training, the most important qualities of a student are native intelligence and the ability to work on his own. Together these qualities mean that he will learn what he needs to learn to pursue his vocation, whatever amount of independent study it requires. Such real education, or learning of self-responsibility, is an attribute which is discouraged by the very organization of schools. But it is entirely conceivable and socially quite achievable to create environments for learning in some of the ways indicated in chapters 5 and 6, that will generate such self-responsibility.

5

Academic Achievement and the Structure of Competition

In secondary education (and to a lesser extent in lower grades), we are beset by a peculiar paradox: in our complex industrial society, there is increasingly more to learn, and formal education is ever more important in shaping one's life chances; at the same time, there is coming to be more and more an independent "society of adolescents," an adolescent culture that shows little interest in education and focuses the attention of teen-agers on cars, dates, sports, popular music, and other matters just as unrelated to school. Thus, while it is becoming more important that teen-agers show a desire to learn, the developing adolescent culture shifts its interest further and further away from learning.

Are these conflicting tendencies "natural" ones, irreversible processes resulting from changes in society? Is the nonchalance of the adolescent culture toward scholastic matters, its irresponsibility and hedonism, simply because "teen-agers are that way"? Is it something that must be accepted? If so, then the hope of developing students truly interested in learning lies in "rescuing" from the adolescent culture a few students who accept adult values, set their sights on long-range goals, and pay little attention to the frivolous activities of their fellows. This approach is very nearly the one we take now, in our emphasis on special programs for "the gifted child," our concern with selecting the most intelligent and setting them apart with special tasks that will further separate them from their fellows.

This is one approach to the problem, but I think a too-simple one, that refuses to face the serious problem of raising the level of training of the less-than-gifted child; this in effect says that we must accept the hedonism and lack of interest in learning of the adolescent culture, a hedonism that drains off the energies of the majority of high school students. This is an approach that can fail even in its attempt to develop the potentials of the gifted child, for it depends completely on the selection process and, at its best, probably misses far more potential scientists and scholars than it discovers.

The question of importance, then, is whether this approach is necessary or whether it might be possible for the school itself, or the community, to modify these values in such a way that they will reinforce, rather than conflict with, educational goals? The first step in answering these questions is to analyze the source of the existing norms of the adolescent culture—to refuse to explain away these values by asserting that "teen-agers are that way," and instead to inquire how the social demands and constraints to which adolescents are subject may help generate these norms.

Institutional Demands and Group Response

There is a class of institutions that are essentially composed of an administrative corps and a larger group of persons subject to such administration. Schools are one such institution, the teachers, of course, being the "administrative corps" and the students subject to their ministrations.

The armed services are another example, the officers and enlisted men composing the two groups. Many factories, which have a great number of workers doing roughly similar tasks under the authority of management, are institutions of this sort.

Jails are perhaps the most extreme example, for in jails the constraints placed on the inmates by the guards are maximal, and there is no period of escape from the demands of the institution.

To be sure, these institutions have many differences. The demands placed on prisoners by the warden, or the demands placed on workers by management, are very different from those placed on teen-agers by the school. Yet the fact remains that the school is an institution designed by the adult society to transmit values and skills to children. To transmit these values and skills, the school makes demands on its students.

In all such institutions, the administrative corps makes certain demands on, and places certain constraints on, those under them. In some institutions, the demands and constraints are great; in others they are less so. A kind of continuum could be conceived, with jails at the one extreme of maximal demands and constraints, the army somewhere in the middle, and schools and factories located farther from the maximal extreme (though differences among schools and differences among factories are so great that both can vary almost from one extreme of the continuum to the other). The demands made by management on workers are essentially that they work and produce, in return for which they receive pay. Similarly, in schools, the demands are that the students study and learn, in return for which they receive grades and are promoted.

The second characteristic of such institutions of importance to the present discussion is not part of the formal rules and regulations and cannot be found in books of standard practice or in the school principal's handbook of administration. Yet it is no less there. This is the collective response to the demands and constraints made by the group on which these demands and constraints are thrust. In jails, the codes and norms to which the inmates hold each other are sharply divergent from the goals and aims of the prison. The fact that prisons do not rehabilitate but largely confirm offenders in criminal ways is almost solely attributable to the fact that each prisoner is subject to the society of the inmates, with its deviant norms and values, and cannot be reached by the professed goals of the prison.[1] It should be noted, however, that not *all* the prisoners adhere to the strong group values and norms of the body of prisoners; some isolates either go wholly their own way or go along with the administration.

The jail is an extreme case, of course. But it illustrates the kinds of process that occur in other institutions. In factories, among groups of workers, the same process has been documented by much research.[2] Work groups develop norms about how much work is "appropriate," norms against working for employers who pay low rates, norms against taking the jobs of men protesting against an employer. The rules of unions against such practices are merely the formalization of these norms.

These norms are reinforced by all the means groups have at their disposal—ridicule, ostracism, loss of prestige, even physical violence. The "rate-buster" is only one of many epithets that serve to set apart the worker who refuses to reduce his pace to meet the norms.[3]

The defensiveness of these work groups of course varies quite radically from industry to industry and employer to employer.

[1] Several interesting researches show the values of the prisoners. A classic is Donald Clemmer's *The Prison Community* (Boston: Christopher, 1940). Richard Cloward, reporting on intensive research in an army prison, shows well the norms that develop among prisoners in response to the demands of the prison. He also shows the different modes of response of different prisoners to the rehabilitative aims of the prison. This is reported in "Social Control in the Prison," *Theoretical Studies of the Social Organization of the Prison*, Bulletin No. 15 (New York: Social Science Research Council, March 1960).

[2] A classic study is F. J. Roethlisberger and W. J. Dickson, *Management and the Worker* (Cambridge: Harvard University Press, 1939). A more recent study of a number of work groups gives considerable insight into the conditions that generate norms of defensiveness among workers. See Leonard R. Sayles, *Behavior of Industrial Work Groups: Prediction and Control* (New York: John Wiley & Sons, Inc., 1958).

[3] This is not to say that there are not sometimes pressures in the opposite direction—to work harder, faster. But these are pressures from the other workers as *individuals*, in the absence of group formation. Peter Blau

The organizations of workers in response to employers' demands range from the most militant unions, with their arsenal of defense weapons, to nonunionized informal work groups who have no dispute with their employer and use only the mildest means to constrain their over-eager fellows. It is true also, as in the jail, that despite the strength of these informal norms among workers, some workers isolate themselves from the group constraints and set their own pace.

The same process that occurs among prisoners in a jail and among workers in a factory is found among students in a school. The institution is different; but the demands are there, and the students develop a collective response to these demands. This response takes a similar form to that of workers in industry—holding down effort to a level that can be maintained by all. The students' name for the rate-buster is the "curve-raiser" or the "D.A.R.—damned average raiser," and their methods of enforcing the work-restricting norms are similar to those of workers—ridicule, kidding, exclusion from the group.

Again it is true that not all the students give in to this group pressure. In particular, scholastically oriented subgroups can form in large schools and insulate their members against the larger group. It is also true that many students, preparing for college, may work intensely in getting ready for a competitive examination for college entrance. Nevertheless, the results of the research discussed above suggest that for most students such intense efforts remain within the framework laid down by the group, interfering little with social activities.

Looking generally now at this class of institutions, it is characterized by demands on the one hand, and group norms resisting

---

shows this well in his *Dynamics of Bureaucracy* (Chicago: University of Chicago Press, 1955), in which he shows one interviewing section in a welfare agency developing group norms that modify the demands on them, while another never develops such norms. Instead, each individual, in direct competition with the others, exerts a pressure for more and faster work.

these demands on the other. What is the source of the group norms? Are they purely a social irrationality, a means by which workers foolishly reduce their own pay, as the employer would argue, a means by which teen-agers impede their own development, as teachers would insist? Hardly so.

Such norms seem quite rational, given a goal of maximum rewards for minimum effort. If the employer sees how much speed is possible, for one man at least, he is likely to revise the work standards upward, or, more informally, to expect more work from the others. Thus the majority is protecting itself from extra work by constraining the fast minority. Since work rates are necessarily relative and cannot be judged except in relation to the rates of other men, then one man's gain is another's loss. Consequently such norms, holding back the fastest men, act as a collective protection, to keep the effort each worker must expend on his job within reasonable bounds.

In a high school, the norms act to hold down the achievements of those who are above average, so that the school's demands will be at a level easily maintained by the majority. Grades are almost completely relative, ranking students relative to others in their class. Thus, extra achievement by one student not only raises his position but lowers the position of others.

Again the response of the group is purely rational. By holding down the efforts and achievements of those who might excel, the general level of effort required to keep an average position is reduced. The group's effort can be seen as one of "combining to prevent excessive competition" and is precisely parallel to the trusts and combines of industries, which attempt by price fixing and other means to prevent excessive competition. The structure of the situation is the same in both cases: the teacher (or the customer) is attempting to deal with each student (or manufacturer) independently, to obtain his best effort (or his lowest price). In response, the students (or manufacturers) combine, placing constraints on one another, so that the effort (or price) may be kept at a level which is comfortable for most members.[4]

With its grading system the school creates what an economist would call a "free-market" situation, with each student a competitor against all his classmates for scholastic position. This unlimited competition, to be sure, may operate without restraint in a few schools, and it is this "free market" that has led some educators and laymen to attempt to reduce competition. In the large majority of schools, however, there is the collective protection, the defense against excessive effort by group norms that restrain efforts. The schools in which such norms do not exist are few indeed. My research included, as mentioned earlier, one elite suburban school from which 85 per cent of the graduates attended college; even in this school, good grades were certainly *not* an important means of prestige, and extra effort devoted to scholastic matters brought on the usual kidding or ridicule. And I also studied a university high school, in which a norm of "good grades without extra effort" exists amid one of the most achievement-oriented student bodies in the country, suggesting that the school's demands seldom fail to create such a response from the adolescent society.

[4] The way in which a modification in the structure of institutional demands and rewards creates a modification in the group response is well illustrated by the following comment. It was written by Jan Hajda, a colleague who had attended a Czechoslovakian gymnasium, on reading a draft of this chapter.

> In the European gymnasium system, both the institutional demands and the group response to them are different. First, the levels of achievement are set by impersonal standards established by the Ministry of Education or a comparable distant supervisory body. Consequently, the standards themselves cannot be manipulated by students nor, for that matter, by their teachers. Theoretically, all students in a given class can pass a course on the highest level or fail to pass. Ideally, the performance of students is judged individually in terms of the set standards and not in comparison with the performance of his peers. This fact tends to minimize—although it does not eliminate—interpersonal competition.
>
> Nobody benefits from holding down effort to a lower level, and consequently there is no reason for protecting the collectivity from superior achievement of a few students. The group solution is not in

These norms produce in students a conflict of motivation: put very simply, to be one of the fellows and not work too hard in school, or to work hard in school and ignore the group. Different teen-agers resolve this conflict in different ways. Whichever way it is resolved, it sets an artificial dichotomy. On the one hand there are sociable average students(who could do far better); on the other hand are a few academically oriented, highly competitive isolates. A boy or (especially) a girl can be oriented to superior achievement *or* to being popular, but it is hard to be both. This is almost puzzling, because in certain activities (e.g., athletics) achievement generates popularity rather than scorn.

The question raised by this situation is whether such a conflict is necessary. Is it impossible to have the group's informal norms positively *reinforce* (or at least not conflict with) scholastic achievement? It is useful to approach the question in a roundabout way, by examining an experiment carried out by a social psychologist some years ago.

Competition versus Cooperation

Morton Deutsch carried out an experiment to show the effects of a "competitive situation" and a "cooperative situation" upon

---

"price-fixing" but in establishing a holding operation which benefits all participants—institutionalized cheating. The informal group norms demand that the top students help the mediocre ones by letting them copy their assignments or by circulating correct answers to a written class examination while the examination is in progress. In a way, the top student is giving up his chance to outdistance others without lowering his own performance. In return, he gets not only recognition for his cooperative behavior but also for his scholastic performance. The better his own performance, the higher the survival chance of his peers.

Thus it is in the interest of the collectivity that there be at least a few outstanding achievers. The top students become symbols of collective security. In turn, academic achievement becomes highly desirable, since it represents the safest way to informal leadership and prestige. The exception to this rule arises only in case the top students refuse to cooperate in cheating, i.e., refuse to share the product of their labors with their peers. In such instances the high achiever is ostracized, ridiculed, and stereotyped as teacher's pet, and his peers do their best to prevent him from making the grade he is aiming for.

achievement, cohesion, and other matters.[6] The experiment went roughly as follows. Classes in industrial psychology were given hypothetical human relations problems to discuss and solve. There were two different reward structures: (1) In some classes, each member was told that he and his four fellow students would each be ranked from one to five according to the contribution of each to the discussion and to the problem's solution. At the end of the semester, each student's grade was based on the average of his ranks through the semester. (2) In five other classes, each class was told that it would be ranked as a class from one to five on the basis of its solution to the problems. At the end of the semester, the ranks of the five classes were averaged, and the members of each class graded according to their class's average rank. Thus in condition (1), each student was being compared with his classmates. In condition (2), each class was being compared with other classes.

Deutsch found several things, all favoring condition (2). He found that the solutions to the problems were better among the classes in condition (2); the class members impeded one another in the discussion under condition (1), but aided one another under condition (2); the feeling of class members toward one another was more positive under condition (2) than (1).

The structure of rewards under conditions (1) and (2) is simple to state: in condition (1), individuals were compared with others in the same group and rewards were relative to these others. This produced competition between individuals. In condition (2), groups were compared with other groups and rewards were relative to the other groups. This produced competition between groups. But although there was competition in both cases, the second kind of competition produced very different consequences from the first in terms of achievement, the group mem-

[6] Morton Deutsch, "The Effects of Cooperation and Competition upon Group Process," in D. Cartwright and A. Zander (eds.), *Group Dynamics* (Evanston: Row Peterson, 1953), pp. 319-53.

bers' feelings toward one another, and in group unity. So long as the group was competing against other groups, one man's achievement benefited, rather than lowered, the position of other members of his group; consequently, the group's response to his achievement was positive rather than negative.

When the competition was between individuals, the fact that one individual's achievement lowered the position of other group members generated interference with one person's efforts by other members, though the interference was perhaps unconscious and subtle. When the competition was between groups, there was support of one person's efforts by others in the group. In effect, then, Deutsch's experiment answers the question raised earlier: whether it is possible for the group's informal rewards to reinforce the formal rewards from the outside. When competition was no longer between individuals, but between groups instead, this reinforcement occurred.

An excellent example of the group's norms reinforcing achievement rather than inhibiting it may be found in the high school itself. Athletics is the activity. In high school athletics, there is no epithet comparable to curve-raiser and no ostracism for too-intense effort for outstanding achievement. Quite to the contrary, the outstanding athlete is the "star," extra effort is applauded by one's fellows, and the informal group rewards are for positive achievement, rather than for restraint of effort.

Why the difference between athletics and studies? The athletic team is competing as a team against another school. Thus, any achievement by one person benefits those around him, who in turn encourage his efforts, rather than discourage them. His efforts benefit the team, and fellow team members encourage his efforts. They bring prestige to the school, and other students encourage and look up to him. His achievements give a lift to the community as a whole, and the community encourages his efforts. The basketball player or aspirant who shoots baskets at lunch period in school is watched with interest and admiration, not with derision. This is in direct opposition to achievement in the classroom, which does not benefit the school and puts one's fellows at a disadvantage. A boy or girl who studies at lunch period is regarded as someone a little odd, or different.

A passage from a novel[7] about a high school illustrates the general process:

> In his home room Trent [a star halfback] received his schedule, made out for him while he was at football camp.
>
> "Are we going to have a good football team this year?" Miss Vereen asked, as she handed him his schedule slip.
>
> "Yes ma'am, I hope so."
>
> "Well, that's fine. That's certainly fine." Miss Vereen knew nothing about football and probably had never seen a game, but anything which increased the stature of Harrison [High School], to which she was fanatically devoted, had her loyal support.

When I wrote to one of the principals in the schools I studied and wanted to say something good or congratulatory about his school, what could I comment on? Nothing scholastic, for his school has little or no opportunity to do anything *as a school* in scholastic directions. I could congratulate him on the basketball team's success, for this is an achievement of the school. When I talked to a class of students and wanted to compliment their school, the same conditions held—I could only congratulate them on what the school had done as a school, which was ordinarily some athletic success in interscholastic competition. Only when talking to one student alone could I congratulate him on his excellent grades.

Such congratulations and support of school activities as a whole, multiplied many times by persons inside and outside the school and the community, encourage a school to do more and better in the directions that bring on such encouragement. Thus, in spite of itself, the school's energies are channeled into these

[7] John Farris, *Harrison High* (New York: Rinehart, 1959), p. 5.

directions that generate support for the school, make others look up to it, and give it pride in itself for its achievements.

One finding from the research discussed earlier is relevant here. The students' school spirit or feeling of identification with the school was indicated by answers to several questions in the questionnaire. It was highest in those schools with winning athletic teams and lowest in schools whose teams had not been successful for several years. But lowest of all was the university high school mentioned earlier, which had a minimal athletic program and discouraged any sort of interscholastic competition. In this school there was seldom an activity the students could "get behind" as a unit.

The peculiar power of interscholastic competition to generate encouragement and support for achievement lies in two directions. First, competition with other groups has a magic ability to create a strong group goal. While some group projects succeed without the added incentive of competition, others would flounder hopelessly were it not for the chance of winning. This has been the fate of many well-intentioned and well-planned group projects in high schools—projects that have failed to capture the energies of the group.

Secondly, interscholastic competition generates support at levels that intergroup competition within the school can never reach. Until now, I have discussed the social support given by other "group members," with no further differentiation. But consider the difference between interscholastic competition, on the one hand, and competition between two teams into which a school class has been divided, on the other. In the latter case, there will be support and encouragement only from fellow team members. In the former case, there wil be support from other team members, from other nonparticipating students, and from persons in the community. That is, if the school's winning gives the community pride in itself and its school, it will encourage team efforts; if the team's winning gives the students pride in their school, they will encourage its efforts.[8]

In other words, when competition is interscholastic, social support and encouragement begin at the level of the school itself, thus permeating the whole social milieu surrounding the team members. When it is intramural, social support begins only at the level of the team, or the subgroup it represents, resulting in a much less supportive social environment for the team member.

An Alternative to Interpersonal Competition

The structure of competition in high schools—interpersonal competition in scholastic matters, interscholastic competition in athletics (and sometimes in music, and occasionally in a few fringe activities)—presents a curious picture. It undermines a student's efforts in scholastic directions (where he is working only for himself), and encourages his efforts in these other, tangential directions (where he is striving for team and school as well as himself). The interests of the adolescent community, emphasizing sports and ignoring studies, must be attributed in large part to this structure of competition—something for which adults, not adolescents, are wholly responsible.

One obvious solution is to substitute interscholastic (and intramural) competition in scholastic matters for the present interpersonal competition for grades. Such a substitution would require a revision of the notion that each student's achievement must be continually evaluated or "graded" in every subject. It would instead make such evaluations infrequent and subsidiary to the group contests and games, both within the school and between schools.

[8] To be sure, there are interscholastic games between schools which are ignored by student body and community alike; but this is less true than is usually realized when such games are given attention and encouragement by the school administration.

Such a change from interpersonal to intergroup competition would also make it necessary to create, with considerable inventiveness, the vehicles for competition: intellectual games, problems, group and individual science projects, and other activities. Yet some examples show that it can be done: debate teams, group discussion tournaments, drama contests, music contests, science fairs (though science fairs as now conducted lack one crucial element, for they are ordinarily competitions between individuals and not between schools, thus lacking the group reinforcement that would go along with "winning for the school"). Math tournaments and speaking contests are other examples of interscholastic competition.

Many examples in high schools show something about the effects such competitions might have. To cite one, a school I studied is too small to compete effectively in most sports, but participates with vigor each year in the state music contests. It nearly always wins a high place in the statewide contest. The striking result of this successful competition is the high status of music among the adolescents themselves. It is a thing of pride to be a trombone soloist in this school, and the leading boys in the school are also the leading musicians—not, as in many schools, scornful of such an unmanly activity. This is despite the fact that the school serves a largely farming community.

It is also true that many of the examples mentioned above have had far less effect in bringing informal social rewards, encouragement, and respect to participants than the present analysis would suggest. The reason is clear, however: such social rewards from the student body as a whole are only forthcoming in response to something the individual or team has done for *them*, such as bringing glory to the school by winning over another school. If the activity, whether it be debate or math competition or basketball, receives no publicity, no recognition in the newspapers and by the community generally, then its winning will have brought little glory to the school, and will bring little encouragement to the participants. (For example, basketball games at the University of Chicago have for years played to crowds of ten or twenty students.)

For this reason, sporadic and infrequent interscholastic competitions in nonathletic activities, with no attention to promotional activity, have little effect. However, if there were systematically organized competitions, tournaments, and meets in all activities ranging from mathematics and English through home economics and industrial arts to basketball and football, and if promotional skills were used, the resulting public and student interest in these activities would undoubtedly increase sharply. Suppose such a set of activities culminated in a "scholastic fair," which, like a state fair, included the most diverse exhibits, projects, competitions, and tournaments, not between individuals, but between schools. I suspect that the impact on student motivation would be remarkably great, because informal social rewards from community and fellow students would reinforce rather than conflict with achievement.

These are simply examples of what might be done to change the structure of rewards in high school—to shift from interpersonal competition, with its conflict-producing effects, to intergroup competition, in which group rewards reinforce achievement. More important than these examples, however, is the general principle that motivations may be sharply altered by altering the structure of rewards and, more particularly, that among adolescents, it is crucial to use the informal group rewards to reinforce the aims of education rather than to impede them.

It is important, of course, to be aware of unintended consequences in changing the reward structure in these suggested ways. For example, in devising interscholastic games of an intellectual sort, it is important that they do in fact teach the skills desired. A carelessly designed program of interscholastic games might result in nothing more than a series of quiz shows, which exercise no other mental activities than those of recall. It is for this reason that the recently developed "political gaming" and "management games," which use electronic computers to simulate the market, seem particularly interesting. Like debate, and unlike quiz shows, these games teach skills and impel the participants to learn how the economic, political, or other system operates.

Perhaps the most important problem in devising such games would be to ensure a balanced system of rewards among the various activities and to ensure a balanced participation among the various students. As many schools have found with extracurricular activities, participation becomes narrowly confined to a few unless rules are set up to prevent such concentration. If interscholastic games were to replace the present within-school competition for grades, such rules to distribute participation would become even more important.

These problems indicate that such changes should be made with care. But the general point is clear: the present structure of rewards in high schools produces a response on the part of the adolescent social system that effectively impedes the process of education. Yet the structure of rewards could be so designed that the adolescent norms themselves would reinforce educational goals.

6

The Nature of Society and the Nature of Education

The Complexity of Society and the Content of Education

When we ask what qualities an adult in society must have, it is useful in answering to think of societies at three points along a continuum of complexity. The first is a communal, face-to-face society in which a man knows personally all the members of his relevant social environment. The second is a society that includes relations at a distance, or what some sociologists call secondary relations. In such societies, a man's daily activities include interactions, both economic and social, with people he does not know personally. A nonindustrial society of craftsmen, merchants, and farmers, spread over a geographic area with travel between different towns, exemplifies the latter type of society. America of the eighteenth and early nineteenth centuries and preindustrialized Europe are concrete cases that illustrate such a society.

The third point on the continuum of complexity is a society that includes, not only primary and secondary relations, but also what might be called tertiary relations: relations with large institutions. Industrialization, the growth of the corporation, and the development of the modern state with all its agencies, have combined to reconstruct society into a vast complex of these organizations, with individuals, qua individuals, in the interstices between them. Many of the activities in the society are activities that involve legal or economic interaction between these large constructs. Many involve primary or secondary relations between people; but many involve relations between people, on the one hand, and these large organizations on the other. In industrial society, finding a job, purchasing, dealing with the law, and registering a political opinion all involve this tertiary form of interaction, that is, not interaction with other people, but with large institutions.

For each of these kinds of society, certain kinds of socialization are necessary for the making of an adult. As the level of complexity increases, the newly needed attributes are not substituted for the ones previously necessary; they are added to them. Thus as the complexity of society increases, the complexity of socialization increases as well.

In the communal, face-to-face society, the basic elements that are necessary for socialization derive directly from the nature of face-to-face relations. An adult must be able to establish relations, develop expectations, and live up to the expectations governing the relation. Two essentials are necessary, one a pure skill and the other a personality attribute. The skill is spoken language; it is necessary to communicate with the other person in order to establish and maintain the relation. The personality attribute may be called the ability to identify with the other. It is the shift from a totally egocentric world, the attribute G. H. Mead called the ability to take the role of the other, the attribute Adam Smith called sympathy in his *Theory of Moral Sentiments*, the attribute we often call empathy today. Whatever it is called, it is the ability to enter into a social interaction, to be governed by it, and to accept the constraints on behavior that such a relationship demands. There are always some persons in society who are not socialized in this way; autistic persons are perhaps the best example.

In the secondary society, which includes relations at a distance, the additional attributes necessary for adequate socialization derive directly from the new form of relation. The skills necessary are those of classical education: the three R's of reading, 'riting, and 'rithmetic. When relations are at a distance, spoken language is no longer sufficient, and direct trading of physical objects is not possible. Written symbols must serve in their place, and mental calculations must replace direct manipulation of objects. Until society includes such relations at a distance, neither written language nor arithmetic calculations are necessary; but when it does, the adult must have these skills in order to perform as a member of society.

The additional skills necessary for occupational performance in such a society derive directly from the new occupations created. For most persons, the occupational skills are no different from those of a communal society; but in addition, the roles of lawyer, teacher, merchant, and others arise, roles that characterize a nonindustrial society of towns and villages. Only in training for these roles is it necessary to go beyond the skills of the three R's.

In such a sociey, the personality attribute necessary is an extension of the ability to identify with others in order to establish a stable personal relation. It is the ability to identify with those whom one has never seen, who are not particular persons, but categories of persons: to realize that those in another town or another nation are not wholly foreign, but behave from motives similar to one's own. It is the ability to recognize as legitimate the interests of those whom one does not know personally, and at the same time to be able to protect one's own interests in such extended relations. It is useful to note that country people are often characterized by two attributes that show the lack of each of these aspects of socialization: suspiciousness of strangers, and gullibility toward sophisticated urbanites. Thus we may say that, just as the primary society requires a shift from a totally *egocentric* world view, the secondary society requires a shift from a totally *ethnocentric* world view. A part of what is called citizenship education in schools today is an attempt to bring about this shift.

Another part of it, however, is an attempt to limit such identification to the borders of the nation. This has always been a function of secondary education: to extend ethnocentricity beyond the family but to focus it at the limits of the nation. Thus extended and focused, the identification provides a unifying force that the nation can use in times of crisis. Such a process is best exemplified by organizations such as the Nazi youth groups, which developed a strong ethnocentricity focused around Germany; but it is evident in much that high schools do. Some elements in secondary education attempt to go beyond such development of national identity, and sometimes succeed; but the frequent reactions by local communities against support of the United Nations have their roots in this nationalizing function of the school.

In the society with tertiary relations, that is, relations with large institutions, the attributes necessary for an adult expand enormously. The skills and the personality attributes required are no longer so clear-cut. It is necessary to perform effectively in relations with these large institutions, which involves such diverse things as obeying formal laws laid down by large governments, knowing how to keep from being cheated in a sale, knowing whether to buy insurance, how to resist advertising, how to find a desirable job, how to make one's voice felt in government, how to handle employers, how to rent or buy a place to live, how to have a telephone installed, how to deal with taxes, and how to use the welfare services provided by the community. To carry out all of these tasks well, an adult in such a society needs many skills and a wide variety of knowledge: greatly increased calculating ability, in order to manage finances and keep from personal bankruptcy; knowledge of where to turn for specific needs; knowledge of the laws, and of the consequences of not obeying them; knowledge of how government operates; an idea of what different jobs are like; and many other such attributes. A boy or girl in such a society faces a vast and complex machinery and is required to deal with parts of that machinery whose sophistication and power (and sometimes cunning) far outweigh his own.

Thus the task of socializing agencies in such a society becomes an extremely difficult one. Some of the tasks are not dealt with through socialization alone: trade unions have developed to deal collectively with employers, consumers' information magazines give product advice, and laws have developed to protect individuals against unscrupulous organizations. But many of the tasks must be carried out as part of socialization.

In all of these kinds of society, we may think of the task of socialization as that of transforming an infant into a "self-regulating" and "self-motivating" entity. Early in life, a child's behavior is totally governed by his parents; and he acts under their authority, both in his constraints and in his positive actions. But when he is an adult in a democratic socety, he must be autonomous, self-regulating, and self-motivating, and must have internalized those aspects of the society with which he will interact. The question of how a society, particularly a complex one composed of large institutions, can bring about this internalization is the critical problem of education.

The Agencies of Socialization

The task of socialization for primary relations is not seen as problematic by any society. Such socialization occurs early in childhood, principally within the family. To be sure, there is an extremely wide range of variation in the quality of socialization that occurs. But until an effective substitute is found for the family in early childhood, it seems unlikely that this range of variation will diminish greatly. Since I foresee no effective substitute, I will note only that, as long as such wide variation does exist, the problem remains how to ensure that primary socialization processes are carried out well.

In contrast to the socialization of primary relations, specific basic skills such as reading, writing, and arithmetic, together with further skills and other aspects of socialization for secondary and tertiary relations are taught in formal institutions and seem likely to remain so. Why is this true? The existence of television and printed media make it technically simple to present to all children in a modern society the same information they now receive from teachers in schools, at a fraction of the cost to the society. Yet there is no suggestion that schools be disbanded and education take place in the home.

This means that there is something important about the schools themselves, apart from the content of the knowledge they present to children. The most obvious added element is the authority that the school has over the child. Without this authority and the schedule of activities imposed on every child, it is easy to conjecture that for many children, little learning would take place. There are many activities more interesting to a child than practicing writing, reading, or addition, when he is left to his own devices.

Yet perhaps the most difficult learning of all, that of speech, is accomplished by these same children, at an earlier age, wholly without the aid of an external institution. Why cannot these simpler skills be learned in the same way? What is it about them that requires the crutch of an institution with compelling authority?

The difference, I think, lies in the different roles that primary and secondary relations play in a child's social behavior. The ability to function in primary relations is necessary to the child from an early age, if it is to cope with its environment at all. For its environment consists of both a physical world and a social world, and that social world consists wholly of face-to-face contacts, requiring spoken language, with a relatively stable set of persons.

The socialization tasks of the school, in contrast, are those concerned with secondary relations, relations at a distance. These relations are not part of a child's everyday existence. He need not write or read or calculate or know about faraway places in order to get along with his family and friends. It is only the artificial demands of the school that make them necessary. He may need these skills as an adult; but as a child, he is still living in a communal society composed of primary relations.

Thus one solution to this problem is to commit children to an institution—to use the authority held by adults to coerce learning of these as yet unimportant activities. It is reasonable, however, to consider other institutional mechanisms. It is evident that many things are wrong with this one solution, which uses adult authority to coerce learning. Perhaps the major defect is that the learning just does not occur very well. Neither the skills nor the internalization of society required for secondary and tertiary relations are well or efficiently learned, as compared to the learning of speech and empathy in primary relations.

If one reflects for a time on the way these early skills are learned, compared to the methods of the schools, he sees certain striking differences. When a child is small, he must learn if he is to stay alive. His energies must be fiercely concentrated toward understanding the world in which he lives, toward becoming what he is not. When he is grown, he may distribute his energies as he sees fit. His security and shelter are often assured; and when they are not, the activities that make them so have little to do with learning. Recently, I saw my young son concentrating intensely on cutting a paper in the shape of a circle. He *must* do that, and he would do it, trying until someday he pulled himself to an "adult" level of competence. In the meantime his father, who could already cut a circle reasonably well, sat, newspaper in hand, mind wandering, eyes scanning, energies dissipated in a multitude of directions. The young son, having to fight his way out of the ignorance and incompetence of childhood, has his energies focused by that fight. The father, having won that battle, can relax his energies.

Somewhere in between is the adolescent—old enough to make his way in the physical world, yet too young to manage the complexities of modern industrial society. He can handle himself in the society of his peers, and, to be sure, in the company of adults as well. A boy can hold a job if he likes, and he can own and drive a car; a girl suddenly finds herself able to hold her own in the world of womanly competition—in the same league with adult women, if she so chooses. And adolescents today have more of the equipment of adult life than ever before. Cars are the most important, but there are other things. Adolescents have become an important market, not only for popular music (where they have always constituted the major part of the audience), but also for movies, which have been directed more and more toward adolescents, since television diverted the mass adult audience. Similarly, for many other commodities, particularly clothes and sporting goods, adolescents now constitute a very important market, with their own considerable buying power. For some years they have even had their own special market researchers, discovering their tastes and weaknesses for wide-awake entrepreneurs.

In short, the adolescent no longer faces the barriers of illiteracy, inarticulateness, and inability to comprehend that focused his energies and forced him to learn as a child. These fundamental hurdles overcome, his energies may spread themselves in the diverse directions toward which our affluent society pulls. For the first time, "learning" has serious competitors for his attention and energy. The primacy of the school can no longer be taken for granted, and formal education must take its place alongside the other activities that compete for an adolescent's energy. If formal education can successfully compete with these other attractions, well and good; but compete it must, for learning no longer has the unquestioned urgency it once had when the child was unable to cut a paper into the shape of a circle.

Not so very long ago in our society, and even yet in most other societies, the natural hurdles offered by the child's environment were quickly followed by others just as natural. Children were thrust into a man's world when they had reached a man's size: they quickly went into an occupation—whether on the farm, or in their father's shop, or as a houseservant—or into academic training for a specific occupation such as law, medicine, ministry, or teaching. In every case, the occupation offered its specific and very obvious hurdles, whether physical or mental, hurdles that continued to focus energies until some security was gained.

These immediate hurdles leading to a specific occupation, which once existed for a boy or girl of fourteen or fifteen, are no longer in evidence. The requirements of industrial society have greatly extended the period of general education, and have created a state of limbo that we know as adolescence. The adolescent is no longer child, not yet adult; he is uncommitted to any specific occupation with its specific hurdles, yet he is "committed" to an institution devoted to educating him. That institution, of course, is the high school.

If that institution is to succeed, it must manage to capture the energies and attention of the inmates who are committed to it. It must compete "in the open market," so to speak, for the energies that are no longer focused on learning by the natural hurdles of the environment. It has some advantages over other competing activities, for it has physical control over adolescents for a large portion of each day; and it has a stamp of approval, in the form of a diploma and records for college admission, which it can give or withhold.

These are important weapons in the competition for adolescent energy, and they are used implicitly or explicitly by every high school, and by every teacher. But these weapons are of a coercive sort, reminding one of the dictum, "You can lead a horse to water, but you can't make him drink." The horse is under the external control of the master, and the adolescent under the external control of the adult, but the horse and the adolescent will drink at their respective fountains only if they want to do so —disdaining the master's or adult's plea that it is in their own interest.

That such external control is not highly effective is obvious to any observer of our society. The casual observer of modern "youth culture" might easily wonder whether these weapons are at all effective in the competition for adolescent energy. Adolescents' lives are filled with many things; their energies flow in many directions; and much as adults may wish that the flow toward learning be great, the hard facts of the case suggest otherwise.

The Open Society and the Structure of Education

In preindustrial society, most persons found themselves confined within a single authority system in a closed society. Each man had his "station" in life. Women could be held in a subordinate position; a man could be held as a slave, an indentured servant, or a serf; the sons of cobblers were content to be cobblers all their life; and children are kept in their place. The prototype of such a society is the household of medieval and postmedieval times. The head of the household was master of all those in it, both responsible for them and in complete authority over them: not only his family members, but any apprentices and workers who might be part of the household. And outside the household, there was a series of levels or estates in society, with each person fixed rigidly in his estate, under the complete authority of the estate above him.[1]

As industrial economy has developed, it has brought with it

[1] Such a hierarchy is so pronounced that the historian, J. Huizinga, in *The Waning of the Middle Ages* (Garden City, N. Y.: Anchor Books, 1956), titles his third chapter "The Hierarchical Conception of Society."

a kind of economic freedom which has "opened up" society and freed these various subject persons from their stations: each man is now a wage laborer, free to sell his talent in an open market; a woman is freed from economic dependency and no longer bound to the household. Children are the last to be freed by the openness of an industrial economy, but they too are no longer content to have a fixed station, to be "seen and not heard." The openness coupled with affluence allows the adolescent to share fully in his family's consumption, and to do so independently: to own a car, to select his own clothes, to spend his time outside school as he sees fit. A steelworker's son aspires to the same jobs and the same style of life as does the company president's son.

An open society creates problems, especially for adolescents. Censorship versus obscene literature provides a good example of such problems: how far should society constrain the purveyors of sexual stimulation in the mass media from focusing on an adolescent audience? Cigarette advertising is another example: despite our knowledge that cigarette advertising is particularly appealing to the adolescent, we are unable to solve the problem of physical harm induced by early smoking. The simple solutions that would legaly restrict adolescents curtail the openness of society and would attempt to coerce behavior. Such other solutions as legally restricting the advertiser are also difficult to apply while still maintaining the openness of society. The open society is still in its infancy, and we have not yet learned how to curb its excesses without sacrificing the openness itself.

The existence of massive poverty and dependence, side by side with affluence, is another consequence of an open society. Despite our high standard of living, no city in Western Europe has the slums that American cities have. This results quite directly from the openness of our society as compared to Europe. In many European countries, an unskilled worker receives most of his income in the form of subsidies for his necessities. His consumption decisions are largely made for him, for his money wages are small. In the United States, he receives most of his income as money wage and thus has control over the consumption decisions. This means he is prey to his own passions and his own ignorance, to the avarice of merchants and to the skill of advertisers. His wages are dissipated without improving his living conditions.

Again this indicates our present inabilities to cope with the consequences of an open society. And again, the simple solution is the totalitarian one: revoke this freedom, and make the consumption decisions for the poor through subsidy for their basic necessities. The solutions consistent with an open society are not so simple, for they involve education and organization, arming the consumer to protect his own interests while maintaining his freedom of choice.

In such a society, the school itself is an anachronism. For students are not at school out of free choice; they are required to attend, and most of their actions in school are dictated as well. A student must attend particular classes under teachers to whom he is assigned; he has a required place to be and required activity at all times during the day. This pattern that characterizes the school was once wholly consistent with the remainder of an adolescent's life; so long as he was within the family, his behavior was under the authority of the family; he had little time or money that he could employ wholly at his own caprice. Now, however, it is the school alone that so sharply restricts his choice. Outside the school, he too is in an open society, with time and money to use as he wishes. As a consequence, the school is at a great disadvantage in capturing the adolescent's interest. If he is eager for adulthood, he is quick to turn his attention to those areas of leisure and consumption that allow him the freedom of an adult.

For some adolescents, of course, the vision of the future has been very sharply etched and its dependence on education made clear. Such adolescents are able to resist the inducements of "immediate adulthood," and subject themselves to the coercion of the classroom. Also, some students receive more day-to-day rewards from their activities in school and find little discrepancy between the activities they are required to carry out and those they would choose themselves. Still others are passive, without the spark of independence. For those adolescents, school proceeds smoothly, and they find little to react against. For others, the open society beckons too insistently to be ignored.

In different social strata, this problem takes different forms, though its fundamental causes are the same. Among the middle classes, it takes the form of attention to fun, pleasure, and excitement: joyrides in sports cars, spring vacations at Fort Lauderdale, surfing, tearing up resort towns on Labor Day weekend, and similar pursuits. For those without money, it may take more consistently antisocial forms: joyrides in stolen cars, gang activities, truancy, and similar activities. For both groups, it includes adoption of styles of life reserved for adults, such as smoking and drinking.

Thus there is a basic incompatibility between an open society for an adolescent and a school with compulsory attendance and required behavior. Such an incompatibility may be resolved in several ways. Each of these alternatives bears serious consideration, so each should be examined in turn.

(1) The first is to take the adolescent from the strains and demands of the open society into a closed community. This has been the characteristic solution of the upper classes in Britain, sending their sons to boarding schools. This allowed the adults to enjoy the fruits of wealth, while placing the children in a spartan environment compatible with classical education. This alternative is also employed by some in the United States, who send their children to boarding schools. This—boarding schools—is an alternative that has never been seriously considered for the society as a whole. It is an alternative that explicitly recognizes an adolescent's inability to cope with the attractions of an

open society and our inability to forearm him against these attractions. For the many adolescents (from the highest to the lowest classes) whose families have psychologically deserted them, it may be that the only workable solution is such a closed community as a boarding school provides.

But there are two kinds of "closed community" in which young people can develop. Briefly, they can be described as communities in which authority comes from without, from the adults who "run" the institutions, and those in which the authority comes from within, from each adolescent and from the communities of adolescents. Either kind can run well or run poorly. And neither, even at its best, prepares fully for life in an open society, with its distractions, tensions, and temptations. But by far the one with most potential in an open society is the one in which authority comes from within. Such a communty is based on the following hypothesis: If every vestige of authority and constraint employed by adults is removed from children, they will no longer react against the constraints but must necessarily set up their own, which then constitute self-regulation. This thesis is based on the premise that most norms and constraints of society (or at least all those that should be transmitted to the young) derive from the necessity of maintaining social order and that children will learn these constraints when they must establish social order among themselves.

This thesis (on which the social therapeutic technique of role-playing also depends) is an eminently reasonable one. From it one would deduce that children learn more about norms and about internalization of the role of the other through their own social games, which break down if the rules are not obeyed, than from their parents, teachers, or other adults.

There is one excellent example of this thesis having been put into practice. The practitioner is A. S. Neill, an Englishman who a number of years ago established a community of children and a school without rules, compulsion, or requirements for attendance.[2] There has never been a serious evaluation of this experiment, but it should be taken quite seriously. The indications are that the hypothesis is correct and that, under certain conditions, the process works. Whether such conditions are compatible with other institutions of modern society is an open question.

Neill's experiment includes a second hypothesis: Without adult compulsion, children will come to learn the attributes required for secondary and tertiary relations, that is, all the things that are "taught" in ordinary schools. If school subjects are available, they will be sought after and learned. The results from Neill's community-school leave considerable doubt that this is true—at least under the conditions that he established. It seems, on the basis of scanty evidence, that as long as these relations are of little importance in children's everyday lives, they do not seek to learn them on their own. As Neill says of his own experiment, the children of Summerhill do not seem much interested in book learning.

This experiment is instructive, for it provides certain of the conditions under which learning can best take place, though not others. That is, it provides an environment in which a boy or girl can be free to learn from his own actions and their consequences. He is not told what he must learn, but neither can he escape from the consequences of his actions, as he often can in his life with the family. For the most important element of this experiment is thc community of children that is established. It is not under external restraint, so it need not develop norms of resistance. To survive, it must itself establish and maintain order.

Neill, along with some others who have set up similar communities, is apparently blind to the existence of social norms, and he attributes the development of maturity to the "complete freedom" which each child has. However, his own description of the community clearly refutes this. The critical difference be-

[2] See A. S. Neill, *Summerhill* (New York: Hart Publishing Co., 1960).

tween this community and a regular school is not the freedom that a child has, for a child is probably freer in the outside society; it is the freedom that the community of children has as a community. Thus what is established is not so much a self-regulating child, but a self-regulating community. The roles of responsibility that a child experiences in such an environment undoubtedly account for the maturity and self-responsibility that the child develops.

The essential lack in a community like Summerhill is the lack of demand. To be sure, the child is free to act and take the consequences of his action. He therefore learns how to behave responsibly in a small, stable, face-to-face community. He need learn nothing more, and apparently does not. (In those instances where Summerhill children do take an active interest in scholastic matters, the motivation apparently comes from the outside world: from the entrance requirements of the institutions they hope to enter. This is no different an activity than "boning up for College Boards" in ordinary schools and deserves no special admiration.)

It is evident that such an environment lacks one essential: the obstacles that induce learning as they are overcome. Summerhill (and other places similar to it) is a warm, close, primary community. To survive within it, one must break out of his egocentrism; but one need not know how to read, write, or calculate. He need learn none of the skills of a tertiary society, none of the ways of getting about in the maze of large organizations of which such a society is composed. He need learn no real economic skills for such a society, since he remains in the warmth of a primary community, only one step removed (though an exceedingly important step) from the family. He does not face the coldness, the harshness, the impersonality, and the freedom of the tertiary society he will live in as an adult. This defect is one that has plagued many of the closed communities constructed for the maturation of adolescents. These communities have few of the attributes of an open, rational society with tertiary relations, and thus leave wide gaps in learning for these societies.[3]

(2) A second alternative resolves the incompatibility between this compulsion and an open society in the opposite direction. Instead of creating a closed community, it would make schools more open and more voluntary in the open society. They would have to compete in an open market, so to speak, for the adolescent's attention. There are several ways this could be done.

One way of opening up the schools would be to have a multitude of components of schools that a boy or girl *could* attend, though no single one was compulsory. Such special purpose "component schools" should be, if they are to be successful, the creation of private enterprises through government contracts. The introduction of competition, if the competitors and the students were paid on the basis of production (that is, measured change produced in their students), might bring a wealth of new ways to learn such basic skills as reading and arithmetic efficiently. And each student could seek out the place that fitted him. Since both student and school were paid as a function of his learning, both would be motivated to work hard to bring about such learning. And in the process, the student would have both the autonomy and the responsibility that he does not now have. He might gain the self-discipline so important to adult life in an open society. The steps toward such a system of competitive component schools are not so difficult as might be supposed. Federal aid to education could take the form of contracts for such schools. Students could attend the component schools for

[3] There is some evidence that suggests that a very different hypothesis may be true, that the source of discipline is not important; rather, it is the fact that the child achieves control of his environment that gives him the ego strength that will lead to further learning. Such conquest can come about either through internal self discipline or through imposed discipline.

part of a day on released time from the public school, thus reducing the pressures in the public school. And both the student and the component school could be paid on the basis of performance.[4]

School, which has always been considered a certain phase or period in an individual's life, must now be considered a lifetime activity. Given this development, the age of compulsory full-time schooling might be lowered, say to fourteen. But then beyond this point, a boy or girl would receive incentives for continued education, on either a part-time or full-time basis, of either an academic or a vocational variety. The incentives would compensate him for the income foregone and thus make it financially, as well as intellectually, interesting for him to learn throughout his life. One precedent for such paid continuing education exists in the active reserve of the Armed Forces. If this can be done for defense against other countries, it can be done as well for defense against obsolescence of skills, joblessness, and a malfunctioning economy.

Simulated Social Environments

If the incompatibility between the openness of society and the authority of the school is to be resolved in the direction of an open system of education, one special difficulty arises. So long as the curriculum of the school and the activities of its students are determined in a closed authority system, the adults at the top of this system can dictate what should be learned and impose actions in this direction. The consequence of failing to learn this or that, or doing poorly in school generally, are sharp-

[4] A variation on this would be for part of the student's pay to be deferred, and only payable as a stipend when he was enrolled in a school beyond high school. The precedent for this is the G.I. Bill of Rights, in which funds for education were "earned" by length of service. This would modify that only by having the funds earned by productivity as well as time, that is, by achievement on standard tests.

ly evident to the adults, who are currently experiencing those consequences.

But when school is "opened up," so that what a boy or a girl learns is his own responsibility, the adults' experiences no longer dictate his course of action. His actions are taken by his own choice, and that choice must be made from his peculiar perspective as an adolescent. From this perspective, he has difficulty seeing consequences far in the future. He sees only current consequences in his everyday life. This shortsighted view leads to a kind of hedonism that characterizes much of modern adolescence. Thus what has been removed is the adult predigested wisdom and the authority to enforce it, and nothing has been substituted for it. What is necessary is a kind of "social telescope" for seeing far-distant consequences vividly enough so that they affect current behavior.

In addition, if the adolescent bereft of adult authority is to make wise choices, he needs to "see into" a variety of roles and activities with which he has had no experience as a child. When he is older, with experience, this wisdom will be his; but the choices will have already been made. He needs a social telescope that will act not only in time, but in space, both to bring future consequences into the present and to bring strange and alien roles into his immediate experience. Clearly this is impossible to carry out fully, for he would need to lead two lives in sequence. But it can be simulated, bringing to him some of the flavor of those far-away situations. This can be done through realistic socioeconomic games to simulate environments that adolescents could not otherwise experience. I have elsewhere written of these games, argued their advantages, and described my research with them, and I will not repeat that discussion here.[5] I will mention only one game which illustrates this well. This is a career game, which begins with a hypothetical boy or girl (having par-

[5] See James S. Coleman, "Collective Decisions," *Sociological Inquiry* (Spring 1964); "Playing Politics in the Classroom," *The Johns Hopkins Magazine* (October 1963).

ticular abilities, family situation and school record) in the tenth grade. The player must first select among various goals in terms of which he wants his person's life to be evaluated. Then he must make decisions, first about courses in school and free time allocation and later about further education, job, marriage, and children. The "environment" in which he makes these decisions corresponds as closely as possible to a real one: curricula found in real high schools and colleges, detailed information from guidance books on job prerequisites and statistics on job opportunities, and so on. The results with this game to date have been striking indeed: players report a far greater sense of the connection between present decisions and future life chances, as well as an awareness of a far greater variety of future jobs. Before–after measurements confirm these reports, but it is the changes which the players perceive in themselves that are most impressive. One girl wrote, after playing the game, "Well, before I think that I felt that women just sort of became what they were. Now I know the amount of planning that goes into a woman's life. The best life for a woman is what she can afford and wants to do for herself. She is the only one who can make up her own mind and do what is best for herself."[6]

This game illustrates one variety of simulated environments. It should be evident that these environments are a response to the special problem of limited perspective that arises when adolescents are given autonomy and responsibility over their learning in a complex society. They are one approach designed to allow young people to acquire the qualities that our complex urban society will require of them. They clearly lack some of the requirements that an autonomous community of adolescents provides. But they are a means by which adolescents can be drawn into the environments and roles they will face as adults. They act in much the same way a Link Trainer acts for a neo-

[6] Sarane S. Boocock, "Simulation Games: Bringing the World into the Classroom," *Vassar Alumnae Magazine*, 49 (1964), 20–22.

phyte pilot. As our ability to devise good environments increases, the richness of insight into self and society they provide will increase. It is clear, of course, that they answer only part of the problem, for they hardly give adolescents a chance for real responsibility and autonomy. But as part of present schools or of the communities of adolescents described above, they constitute an important aid in acquainting the adolescent with the complex world of his future.

The Ideal Learning Environment

The following requirements might be set down as a model for a learning environment.

(1) An individual must have the freedom and opportunity to carry out his own actions and make his own mistakes.

(2) The environment must be so structured as to allow him to experience the mistakes as mistakes, to feel the consequences of his actions. (One of the major defects of an adolescent's "natural" environment in modern society is that he can easily escape the consequences of his actions. Such environments are not neutral, but rather give positive encouragement to irresponsibility.)

(3) The actions must be relatively small, inconsequential, and endlessly repeatable, so that the consequences are not so severe as to discourage action and his successes outnumber his failures.

(4) The environment must provide obstacles that, in being overcome, induce the desired learning. That is, it must not be possible to survive in such an environment without learning the desired skills.[7] In learning for tertiary societies, these skills include a variety of social roles in which the individual must learn to perform if he is to function in such societies.

[7] Learning to speak a foreign language illustrates well the necessity for such obstacles. The pain of learning is so great that if the environment includes a haven, such as the possibility to converse in one's native tongue, nearly all persons will retire into it and learn only very slowly, if at all. But denied such a haven, learning proceeds because it must if the individual is to survive in this linguistic environment.

This fourth point is a critical one, because idealists in education, concerned with establishing a supportive environment, often neglect the fact that a supportive environment gives no inducement to learning. Such an environment may be beneficial to the child's present through its supportiveness; but by not exposing him, under relatively safe circumstances, to those conditions about which he must learn for later life, it is inimical to his future.

These four elements (of which all but the fourth are missing in traditional education, while the fourth is missing in progressive education) appear to be the critical ones in an environment designed for learning. The general hypothesis on which the idea of learning environments is based can be stated as follows: A child will learn those things he must learn to perform effectively in his present environment. He will not learn things that will only be useful in the far future, for he cannot project himself into future roles and activities. The construction of such learning environments would involve bringing future roles into the present and requiring a child to perform in these roles, rather than merely in those that naturally befall him as a child or adolescent.

Although progressive education does not conform to the four points stated above, this thesis is akin to Dewey's thesis of "bringing the community into the school," making of the school a microcosmic community.[8] The extracurricular activities of many high schools constitute a movement in this direction. The results of these extracurricular developments are ambiguous. It is quite clear that some things have gone as expected: work on a school newspaper has led many boys into careers of journalism and made many other adolescents far more aware of the functioning of society than they might otherwise have been.

[8] Another way of stating the principal defect of Dewey's thesis, compared to the ideal learning environment described above, is that the "community" which was to be brought into the school was a close, warm, primary community, with few of the attributes of the open society with tertiary relations which the child would face as an adult.

But other such activities have led away from the development of responsible adults or been irrelevant to it, though they may be the most sought-after positions in the school community (for example, cheerleader, prom queen, fraternity member). In many schools, the "community of adolescents" (which the school has become) has many of the worst qualities of small ingrown communities of adults: tightly knit and exclusive cliques, a powerful status system, ridiculing of certain useful or harmless activities, and worshipping of others. In addition, it has certain undesirable features of its own, such as rigid norms that may be set up to disrupt the order imposed by adults rather than establish order. In sum, it can hardly be said that such elaboration of the school has worked well; yet this does not negate the hypothesis on which the elaboration is based, for little attention has been given to the establishment of such environments, beyond making them unstructured and supportive. It seems likely that sociology can make important contributions to education in precisely this area: designing the kind of educational environments in which the attributes of secondary and tertiary relations can be learned.

Perhaps the single most crucial quality that must be learned for such societies is self-responsibility. In a society of tertiary relations, a man is alone, on his own, in a way that he never was in a communal society, where the master of the household was responsible for all. Our tertiary society, with its freedom and its mobility, requires of each man that he attend to his own interests, that he be autonomous and responsible for himself.[9] Yet a school is in its very essence precisely the wrong environment for encouraging self-responsibility. Because it is confining and compulsory, school leaves little room for self-responsibility and instead invites its opposite.

[9] This may well be a major reason, in addition to racial discrimination, why American Negroes have had so much more difficult a time adjusting to an urban society than have other immigrant groups—they have so recently left an environment in which they had neither authority over nor responsibility for their own destiny. The feudal social structure of the rural South may have failed to give them the resources necessary for living in an open society.

Environments that generate self-responsibility have been created sporadically in a few private schools, in summer work camps, and elsewhere, such as the Peace Corps. The examples are frequent enough to show that it can be done, yet not frequent enough to have a significant impact on our educational system and on the generations of adolescents who flow through it. But the problems of the present system have become so serious that solutions that once appeared radical now bear serious consideration. Perhaps the most radical is the most fundamental: the creation of ideal learning environments, either through opening up the schools within the open society, or the creation of self-responsible communities of adolescents, not sporadically in a few private schools, but broadly in public education.

The inadequacy of adolescents' present environments becomes apparent from two sides. In the affluent upper middle classes, the family–school environment gives adolescents freedom without the opportunity for responsibility. It thus invites irresponsibility and generates an adolescent community with norms that pull away from learning. In the lowest classes, the compliance demanded by the school conflicts with the rest of a child's environment, and his best solution may be to escape to the streets at the earliest moment.

The requirements for such self-responsible communities are clear. Whether adolescents commute to them or live in them, they must be relatively autonomous communities, with the possibility of community goals as well as the environments for learning secondary and tertiary relations. The creation of an ideal learning environment by opening up the schools in the open society itself is probably much more difficult to accomplish, though some of the initial directions are straightforward.

In sum, there is one most fundamental point: until we bring about a radical reformation of the environment in which the adolescent lives, we cannot expect an adequate solution of the problems posed for adolescents in our society.

Acknowledgments

Chapter 2 was adapted from "Style and Substance in American High Schools," *College Admissions 6: The American Secondary School* (New York: College Entrance Examination Board, 1959).

Chapter 3 was adapted from "Athletics in High Schools," *Annals of the American Academy of Political and Social Science*, 338 (November 1961), 33–43.

Chapter 4 was adapted from "Surplus Youth: A Future without Jobs," *The Nation* (May 25, 1963); "Alternatives for Joblessness," *American Child*, 46, No. 3 (1964), 12–16. (*American Child* is published by the National Committee on Employment of Youth, at 145 East Thirty-second Street, New York, New York 10010.)

Chapter 5 was adapted from "Academic Achievement and the Structure of Competition," *Harvard Educational Review*, 29 (1959), No. 4.

Chapter 6 was adapted from "The Competition for Adolescent Energies," *Phi Delta Kappan* (March 1961); "The Coming Crisis in Secondary Education," *Bulletin of the National As-*

sociation of Secondary-School Principals (February 1965) (Reprinted by permission; copyright: Washington, D.C.); "Research in Autonomy and Responsibility in Adolescents," *Journal of the National Association of Women Deans and Counselors*, 28 (1964), No. 1.

Index